Tapas

a collection of over 100 essential recipes

This edition published in 2010 for Index Books Ltd
LOVE FOOD is an imprint of Parragon Books Ltd

Parragon
Queen Street House
4 Queen Street
Bath BA1 1HE, UK

ISBN: 978-1-4454-0759-3

Printed in China

Internal Design by Terry Jeavons & Company

Notes for the Reader
This book uses both metric and imperial measurements. Follow the same units of measurement throughout; do not mix metric and imperial. All spoon measurements are level: teaspoons are assumed to be 5 ml, and tablespoons are assumed to be 15 ml. Unless otherwise stated, milk is assumed to be full fat, eggs and individual vegetables are medium, and pepper is freshly ground black pepper.

The times given are an approximate guide only. Preparation times differ according to the techniques used by different people and the cooking times may also vary from those given. Optional ingredients, variations or serving suggestions have not been included in the calculations.

Recipes using raw or very lightly cooked eggs should be avoided by infants, the elderly, pregnant women, convalescents and anyone suffering from an illness. Pregnant and breastfeeding women are advised to avoid eating peanuts and peanut products. Sufferers from nut allergies should be aware that some of the ready-made ingredients used in the recipes in this book may contain nuts. Always check the packaging before use.

Picture Acknowledgements
The publisher would like to thank Owen Franken/Corbis for permission to reproduce copyright material for the front cover.

Tapas

introduction

Tapas has become a bit of a buzzword in the last few years, but what exactly is tapas, and where does it come from?

Tapas is the collective name for small, delicious mouthfuls of something savoury, served with a chilled white wine, beer or sherry. It comes from tapa, the Spanish word for lid – specifically, the 'lid' created by the slice of bread that an innkeeper would thoughtfully place on top of a customer's wine glass to keep out the flies and dust between sips. The Andalucians then came up with the idea of balancing a morsel of something tasty on top of the bread to nibble on – a few cubes of cheese or ham – and a new Spanish institution was born.

Today, tapas are served in almost every bar throughout Spain. Usually they are displayed on the bar, and the waiter puts your selection on a plate, for eating either standing up or seated at the bar or a table.

Everything about tapas, from the preparation to eating and enjoying it, is a uniquely Spanish experience. Tapas are what eating is all about, a true feast for the senses – they look and smell delectable and taste even better. Serve them on pretty plates in bright colours to bring a little Spanish sunshine to a cloudy day.

How you use tapas is up to you. A simple selection of these bite-size gastronomic glories can be served with drinks before lunch or dinner, or an array of dishes can make an informal lunch or dinner in themselves. Tapas are made from a wonderful variety of foods – meat, seafood, eggs, nuts and cheese, as well as every vibrant vegetable imaginable, in healthy Mediterranean style, with dips and sauces to add yet more flavour and interest to the tapas experience.

Eating tapas goes hand-in-hand with hospitality, friendship and plenty of good conversation, so tuck in, forget the cares of the day and linger, Spanish-style, with your favourite people.

nibbles

The Spanish have succeeded in elevating pre-lunch or dinner drinks and nibbles to irresistible heights. Succulent green and black olives marinated in herb- and spice-flavoured oil, crunchy roasted almonds coated in coarse sea salt and smoky paprika, bite-size tarts and pizzas, sizzling prawns, chunks of juicy steak or chorizo, dips that taste of pure sunshine, stuffed tomatoes, asparagus spears wrapped in Serrano ham, the must-have ingredient for a Spanish-themed party – the recipes are all here, and all you need to do is choose what you are going to drink as you tuck in and let your imagination take you to another land.

Cocktail sticks are an essential tool when it comes to eating tapas, so provide plenty. In some Spanish bars, all the tapas are served on cocktail sticks, and the number of sticks you leave behind determines the size of your bill – but if you are serving tapas at a party, your objective in providing cocktail sticks is to keep your guests' hands as clean as possible, because eating these tasty morsels can become a very messy business!

If you are planning to serve marinated olives, remember to prepare these ahead of time, because they benefit from being steeped in their flavourings for a day or two, or even longer.

olives with orange & lemon

ingredients

SERVES 4–6

2 tsp fennel seeds

2 tsp cumin seeds

225 g/8 oz green olives

225 g/8 oz black olives

2 tsp grated orange rind

2 tsp grated lemon rind

3 spring onions, finely
    chopped

pinch of ground cinnamon

4 tbsp white wine vinegar

5 tbsp olive oil

2 tbsp orange juice

1 tbsp chopped fresh mint

1 tbsp chopped fresh parsley

method

1 Dry-fry the fennel seeds and cumin seeds in a small, heavy-based frying pan, shaking the pan frequently, until they begin to pop and give off their aroma. Remove the pan from the heat and set aside to cool.

2 Place the olives, orange and lemon rind, spring onions, cinnamon and toasted seeds in a bowl.

3 Whisk the vinegar, olive oil, orange juice, mint and parsley together in a bowl and pour over the olives. Toss well, then cover and allow to chill for 1–2 days before serving.

cracked marinated olives

ingredients

SERVES 8

450 g/1 lb can or jar unpitted
    large green olives, drained
4 garlic cloves, peeled
2 tsp coriander seeds
1 small lemon
4 sprigs of fresh thyme
4 feathery stalks of fennel
2 small fresh red chillies
    (optional)
pepper
Spanish extra-virgin olive oil,
    to cover

method

1 To allow the flavours of the marinade to penetrate the olives, place the olives on a cutting board and, using a rolling pin, bash them lightly so that they crack slightly. Alternatively, use a sharp knife to cut a lengthways slit in each olive as far as the stone. Using the flat side of a broad knife, lightly crush each garlic clove. Using a pestle and mortar, crack the coriander seeds. Cut the lemon, with its rind, into small chunks.

2 Put the olives, garlic, coriander seeds, lemon chunks, thyme sprigs, fennel and chillies, if using, in a large bowl and toss together. Season with pepper to taste, but you should not need to add salt as preserved olives are usually salty enough. Pack the ingredients tightly into a glass jar with a lid. Pour in enough olive oil to cover the olives, then seal the jar tightly.

3 Allow the olives to stand at room temperature for 24 hours, then marinate in the refrigerator for at least 1 week but preferably 2 weeks before serving. From time to time, gently give the jar a shake to remix the ingredients. Return the olives to room temperature and remove from the oil to serve. Provide cocktail sticks for spearing the olives.

olives wrapped with anchovies

ingredients

MAKES 12

12 anchovy fillets in oil, drained

24 pimiento-stuffed green olives in oil, drained

method

1 Using a sharp knife, halve each anchovy fillet lengthways.

2 Wrap a half fillet around the middle of each olive, overlapping the ends, and secure with a wooden cocktail stick. Repeat with another olive and anchovy fillet half and slide onto the cocktail stick. Continue until all the ingredients have been used. Serve immediately or cover until required.

paprika-spiced almonds

ingredients

MAKES 500 G/1 LB 2 OZ
SERVES 4–6

1¹⁄₂ tbsp coarse sea salt

¹⁄₂ tsp smoked sweet Spanish
  paprika, or hot paprika,
  to taste

500 g/1 lb 2 oz blanched
  almonds

extra-virgin olive oil

method

1 Preheat the oven to 200°C/400°F. Place the sea salt and paprika in a mortar and grind with the pestle to a fine powder. Alternatively, use a mini spice blender (the amount is too small to process in a full-size processor).

2 Place the almonds on a baking sheet and toast in the preheated oven for 8–10 minutes, stirring occasionally, until golden and giving off a toasted aroma. Watch after 7 minutes because they burn quickly. Pour into a heatproof bowl.

3 Drizzle over 1 tablespoon of olive oil and stir to ensure all the nuts are lightly and evenly coated. Add extra oil if necessary. Sprinkle with the salt and paprika mixture and stir again. Transfer to a small bowl and serve at room temperature.

salted almonds

ingredients

SERVES 6–8

225 g/8 oz whole almonds, in
their skins or blanched
(see method)
4 tbsp Spanish olive oil
coarse sea salt
1 tsp paprika or ground
cumin (optional)

method

1 Preheat the oven to 180°C/350°F. Fresh almonds in their skins are superior in taste but blanched almonds are much more convenient. If the almonds are not blanched, put them in a bowl, cover with boiling water for 3–4 minutes, then plunge them into cold water for 1 minute. Drain them well in a sieve, then slide off the skins between your fingers. Dry the almonds well on kitchen paper.

2 Put the olive oil in a roasting tin and swirl it round so that it covers the bottom. Add the almonds and toss them in the pan so that they are evenly coated in the oil, then spread them out in a single layer.

3 Roast the almonds in the oven for 20 minutes or until they are light golden brown, tossing several times during the cooking. Drain the almonds on kitchen paper, then transfer them to a bowl.

4 While the almonds are still warm, sprinkle with plenty of sea salt and the paprika or cumin, if using, and toss well together to coat. Serve the almonds warm or cold. The almonds are at their best when served freshly cooked so, if possible, cook them on the day you plan to eat them. However, they can be stored in an airtight container for up to 3 days.

moorish broad bean dip

ingredients

SERVES 6

500 g/1 lb 2 oz shelled fresh
or frozen broad beans

5 tbsp olive oil

1 garlic clove, finely chopped

1 onion, finely chopped

1 tsp ground cumin

1 tbsp lemon juice

175 ml/6 fl oz water

1 tbsp chopped fresh mint

salt and pepper

paprika, to garnish

raw vegetables, crusty bread
or breadsticks, to serve

method

1 If using fresh broad beans, bring a large saucepan of lightly salted water to the boil. Add the beans, then reduce the heat and simmer, covered, for 7 minutes. Drain well, then refresh under cold running water and drain again. Remove and discard the outer skins. If using frozen beans, allow them to thaw completely, then remove and discard the outer skins.

2 Heat 1 tablespoon of the olive oil in a frying pan. Add the garlic, onion and cumin and cook over low heat, stirring occasionally, until the onion is softened and translucent. Add the broad beans and cook, stirring frequently, for 5 minutes.

3 Remove the frying pan from the heat and transfer the mixture to a food processor or blender. Add the lemon juice, the remaining olive oil, water and mint and process to a paste. Season to taste with salt and pepper.

4 Scrape the paste back into the frying pan and heat gently until warm. Transfer to individual serving bowls and dust lightly with paprika. Serve with dippers of your choice.

aubergine & pepper dip

ingredients

SERVES 6–8

2 large aubergines

2 red peppers

4 tbsp Spanish olive oil

2 garlic cloves,
   roughly chopped

grated rind and juice
   of $1/2$ lemon

1 tbsp chopped coriander,
   plus extra sprigs to garnish

$1/2$–1 tsp paprika

salt and pepper

bread or toast, to serve

method

1 Prick the skins of the aubergines and peppers all over with a fork and brush with 1 tablespoon of the olive oil. Place on a baking sheet and bake in a preheated oven, 190°C/375°F, for 45 minutes or until the skins are beginning to turn black, the flesh of the aubergines is very soft and the peppers are deflated.

2 Place the cooked vegetables in a bowl and cover tightly with a clean, damp tea towel. Allow to stand for about 15 minutes or until cool enough to handle, then cut the aubergines in half lengthways, carefully scoop out the flesh and discard the skin. Cut the aubergine flesh into large chunks. Remove and discard the stem, core and seeds from the peppers and cut the flesh into large pieces.

3 Heat the remaining olive oil in a frying pan. Add the vegetables and cook for 5 minutes. Add the garlic and cook for 30 seconds.

4 Drain the contents of the frying pan on kitchen paper, then transfer to a food processor. Add the lemon rind and juice, the chopped coriander, the paprika, and salt and pepper to taste, then process until a speckled purée is formed. Transfer the dip to a serving bowl. Serve warm or at room temperature. Garnish with coriander sprigs and accompany with bread or toast.

aubergine dip

ingredients

SERVES 6–8

1 large aubergine,
    about 400 g/14 oz

5 tbsp olive oil

2 scallions, finely chopped

1 large garlic clove, crushed

2 tbsp finely chopped
    fresh parsley

salt and pepper

smoked sweet Spanish paprika,
    to garnish

French bread, to serve

method

1 Heat 4 tablespoons of the olive oil in a large frying pan over medium-high heat. Add the aubergine slices and cook on both sides until soft and beginning to brown. Remove from the frying pan and allow to cool. The slices will release the oil again as they cool.

2 Heat the remaining olive oil in the frying pan. Add the scallions and garlic and cook for 3 minutes or until the scallions become soft. Remove from the heat and reserve with the aubergine slices to cool.

3 Transfer all the ingredients to a food processor and process just until a coarse purée forms. Transfer to a serving bowl and stir in the parsley. Taste and adjust the seasoning, if necessary. Serve immediately, or cover and allow to chill until 15 minutes before required. Sprinkle with paprika and serve with French bread.

potato wedges with roasted garlic dip

ingredients

SERVES 8

1.3 kg/3 lb potatoes,
    unpeeled and halved
2 tbsp olive oil
1 garlic clove, finely chopped
2 tsp salt

roasted garlic dip

2 garlic bulbs, separated
    into cloves
1 tbsp olive oil
5 tbsp sour cream or
    thick natural yogurt
4 tbsp mayonnaise
salt
paprika, to taste

method

1 To make the roasted garlic dip, preheat the oven to 200°C/400°F. Place the garlic cloves in an ovenproof dish, then pour in the olive oil and toss to coat. Spread out in a single layer and roast in the preheated oven for 25 minutes or until tender. Remove from the oven and set aside until cool enough to handle.

2 Peel the garlic cloves, then place on a heavy cutting board and sprinkle with a little salt. Mash well with a fork until smooth. Scrape into a bowl and stir in the sour cream and mayonnaise. Season to taste with salt and paprika. Cover the bowl with clingfilm and allow to chill until ready to serve.

3 To cook the potatoes, cut each potato half into 3 wedges and place in a large bowl. Add the olive oil, garlic and salt and toss well. Transfer the wedges to a roasting tin, then arrange in a single layer and roast in the preheated oven for 1–1 1/4 hours or until crisp and golden.

4 Remove from the oven and transfer to serving bowls. Serve immediately, handing round the roasted garlic dip separately.

courgette fritters with pine nut sauce

ingredients

SERVES 8

450 g/1 lb baby courgettes

3 tbsp plain flour

1 tsp paprika

1 large egg

2 tbsp milk

corn oil, for pan-frying

coarse sea salt

pine nut sauce

100 g/3$\frac{1}{2}$ oz pine nuts

1 garlic clove, peeled

3 tbsp Spanish extra-virgin
    olive oil

1 tbsp lemon juice

3 tbsp water

1 tbsp chopped fresh
    flat-leaf parsley

salt and pepper

method

1 Put the pine nuts and garlic in a food processor and blend to form a purée. With the motor still running, gradually add the olive oil, lemon juice and water to form a smooth sauce. Stir in the parsley and season to taste with salt and pepper. Turn into a serving bowl.

2 To prepare the courgettes, cut them on the diagonal into thin slices about 5 mm/$\frac{1}{4}$ inch thick. Put the flour and paprika in a plastic bag and mix together. Beat the egg and milk together in a large bowl.

3 Add the courgette slices to the flour mixture and toss well until coated. Shake off the excess flour. Pour enough corn oil into a large, heavy-based frying pan for a depth of about 1 cm/$\frac{1}{2}$ inch and heat. Dip the courgette slices, one at a time, into the egg mixture, then slip them into the hot oil. Cook the courgette slices, in batches of a single layer, for 2 minutes or until crisp and golden brown.

4 Using a slotted spoon, remove the courgette fritters from the frying pan and drain on kitchen paper. Continue until all the courgette slices have been cooked.

5 Serve the courgette fritters piping hot, lightly sprinkled with sea salt. Accompany with the pine nut sauce.

bandilleras

ingredients

SERVES 8–10

1 tbsp white wine vinegar

4 garlic cloves, finely chopped

1 fresh red chilli, deseeded
    and finely chopped

1 tbsp sweet paprika

4 tbsp olive oil

3 skinless, boneless chicken
    breasts, cut into 2.5-cm/
    1-inch cubes

1 avocado

3 tbsp lemon juice

115 g/4 oz San Simon or
    other smoked cheese, diced

8–10 black olives, pitted

8–10 cherry tomatoes

85 g/3 oz Manchego or
    Cheddar cheese, cubed

8–10 pimiento-stuffed
    green olives

1/2 cantaloupe melon,
    deseeded

5–6 slices serrano ham

picada

4 garlic cloves, finely chopped

6 tbsp chopped fresh parsley

6 tbsp pickled cucumber,
    finely chopped

150 ml/5 fl oz olive oil

method

1 Mix the vinegar, garlic, chilli, paprika and olive oil together in a bowl. Add the chicken and stir well to coat, then cover and allow to marinate in the refrigerator for at least 2 hours or preferably overnight.

2 Heat a large, heavy-based frying pan. Tip the chicken mixture into the pan and cook over low heat, stirring frequently, for 10–15 minutes or until cooked through. Remove from the heat and allow to cool to room temperature, then spear the chicken pieces with wooden cocktail sticks.

3 Peel and stone the avocado and cut into bite-size cubes. Toss in the lemon juice, then thread onto wooden cocktail sticks with the smoked cheese. Thread the black olives, tomatoes, Manchego cheese and stuffed olives onto wooden cocktail sticks.

4 Scoop out 20 balls from the melon with a melon baller or teaspoon. Cut the ham into 20 strips and wrap around the melon balls. Thread the melon balls in pairs onto wooden cocktail sticks.

5 To make the picada, mix all the ingredients together in a bowl until thoroughly combined into a fairly thick paste. Arrange all the filled cocktail sticks – bandilleras – on a large serving platter and serve with bowls of picada.

roasted asparagus with serrano ham

ingredients

MAKES 12

2 tbsp Spanish olive oil

6 slices serrano ham

12 asparagus spears

coarse sea salt

pepper

aïoli (see page 70), to serve

method

1 Preheat the oven to 200°C/400°F. Place half the olive oil in a roasting tin that will hold the asparagus spears in a single layer and swirl it around so that it covers the base. Cut each slice of serrano ham in half lengthways.

2 Trim and discard the coarse woody ends of the asparagus spears, then wrap a slice of ham around the stem end of each spear. Place the wrapped spears in the prepared roasting tin and lightly brush with the remaining olive oil. Season the asparagus with the sea salt and pepper.

3 Roast the asparagus spears in the preheated oven for 10 minutes, depending on the thickness of the asparagus, until tender but still firm. Do not overcook the asparagus spears, as it is important that they are still firm so that you can pick them up with your fingers.

4 Serve the roasted asparagus piping hot, accompanied by a bowl of aïoli for dipping.

ham-wrapped potatoes

ingredients

SERVES 4

12 new potatoes, unpeeled

2 tbsp olive oil

12 slices serrano ham

salt

method

1 Preheat the oven to 200°C/400°F. Place the potatoes in a steamer set over a saucepan of boiling water. Cover and steam for 30 minutes or until tender. Remove from the heat and allow to cool slightly.

2 Pour the olive oil into an ovenproof dish. Wrap each potato in a slice of ham and arrange in the dish in a single layer. Roast in the preheated oven, turning occasionally, for 20 minutes.

3 Transfer the potatoes to warmed serving dishes. Season to taste with salt and either serve immediately or allow to cool a little.

spicy chicken livers

ingredients

SERVES 4–6

115 g/4 oz plain flour

$^1/_2$ tsp ground cumin

$^1/_2$ tsp ground coriander

$^1/_2$ tsp paprika

$^1/_4$ tsp freshly grated nutmeg

salt and pepper

350 g/12 oz chicken livers

6 tbsp olive oil

fresh mint sprigs, to garnish

method

1 Sift the flour onto a large, shallow plate and stir in the cumin, coriander, paprika and nutmeg. Season to taste with salt and pepper.

2 Trim the chicken livers and pat dry with kitchen paper. Cut the livers in halves or quarters. Toss them in the seasoned flour, a few pieces at a time, shaking off any excess.

3 Heat the olive oil in a large, heavy-based frying pan. Cook the livers in batches over high heat, stirring frequently, for 3–5 minutes or until crisp on the outside but still tender in the centre. Serve impaled on wooden cocktail sticks and garnished with mint sprigs.

chicken wings with tomato dressing

ingredients

SERVES 6

175 ml/6 fl oz olive oil

3 garlic cloves, finely chopped

1 tsp ground cumin

1 kg/1 lb 4 oz chicken wings

2 tomatoes, peeled, deseeded and diced

5 tbsp white wine vinegar

1 tbsp shredded fresh basil leaves

method

1 Preheat the oven to 180°C/350°F. Mix 1 tablespoon of the oil, the garlic and the cumin together in a shallow dish. Cut off and discard the tips of the chicken wings and add the wings to the spice mixture, turning to coat. Cover with clingfilm and leave to marinate in a cool place for 15 minutes.

2 Heat 3 tablespoons of the remaining oil in a large, heavy-based frying pan. Add the chicken wings in batches and cook, turning frequently, until golden brown. Transfer to a roasting tin. Roast the chicken wings for 10–15 minutes or until tender and the juices run clear when the point of a sharp knife is inserted into the thickest part of the meat.

3 Meanwhile, mix the remaining olive oil with the tomatoes, vinegar and basil in a bowl.

4 Using tongs, transfer the chicken wings to a non-metallic dish. Pour the dressing over them, turning to coat. Cover with clingfilm, leave to cool, then chill for 4 hours. Remove from the refrigerator 30–60 minutes before serving, to return them to room temperature.

garlic pan-fried bread & chorizo

ingredients

SERVES 6–8

200 g/7 oz chorizo sausage,
    outer casing removed

4 thick slices 2-day-old
    country bread

Spanish olive oil, for pan-frying

3 garlic cloves, finely chopped

2 tbsp chopped fresh
    flat-leaf parsley

paprika, to garnish

method

1 Cut the chorizo sausage into 1-cm/^{1}/$_2$-inch thick slices and cut the bread, with its crusts still on, into 1-cm/^{1}/$_2$-inch cubes. Add enough olive oil to a large, heavy-based frying pan so that it generously covers the bottom. Heat the oil, add the garlic and cook for 30 seconds– 1 minute or until lightly browned.

2 Add the bread cubes to the frying pan and pan-fry, stirring all the time, until golden brown and crisp. Add the chorizo slices and pan-fry for 1–2 minutes or until hot. Using a slotted spoon, remove the bread cubes and chorizo from the frying pan and drain well on kitchen paper.

3 Turn the pan-fried bread and chorizo into a warmed serving bowl, add the chopped parsley and toss together. Garnish the dish with a sprinkling of paprika and serve warm. Accompany with cocktail sticks so that a piece of sausage and a cube of bread can be speared together for eating.

steak bites with chilli sauce

ingredients

SERVES 4–6

2 tbsp olive oil

1 onion, chopped

1 tsp paprika

1 garlic clove, finely chopped

1 fresh red chilli,
    deseeded and sliced

400 g/14 oz canned
    chopped tomatoes

2 tbsp dry white wine

1 tbsp tomato purée

1 tbsp sherry vinegar

2 tsp sugar

2 rump steaks, about
    175–225 g/6–8 oz each

salt and pepper

2 tsp Tabasco sauce

1 tbsp chopped fresh parsley

method

1 Heat half the olive oil in a heavy-based saucepan. Add the onion and cook over low heat, stirring occasionally, for 5 minutes or until softened. Add the paprika, garlic and chilli and cook for an additional 2–3 minutes, then stir in the tomatoes with their juices, wine, tomato purée, vinegar and sugar. Simmer gently for 15–20 minutes or until thickened.

2 Meanwhile, heat a heavy-based frying pan or griddle pan over high heat and brush with the remaining olive oil. Season the steaks to taste with pepper and rub with the Tabasco, then add to the pan or griddle. Cook for 1–1$\frac{1}{2}$ minutes on each side, or until browned. Reduce the heat and cook, turning once, for 3 minutes for rare, 4–5 minutes for medium or 5–7 minutes for well done. Remove from the heat and keep warm.

3 Transfer the sauce to a food processor or blender and process until fairly smooth. Transfer to a serving bowl, then season to taste with salt and pepper and stir in the parsley.

4 Transfer the steaks to a cutting board and cut into bite-size pieces. Impale on wooden cocktail sticks, then place on serving plates and serve immediately with the sauce.

sizzling chilli prawns

ingredients

SERVES 8

500 g/1 lb 2 oz raw king
prawns, in their shells

1 small fresh red chilli

6 tbsp Spanish olive oil

2 garlic cloves, finely chopped

pinch of paprika

salt

crusty bread, to serve

method

1 To prepare the prawns, pull off their heads. With your fingers, peel off their shells, leaving the tails intact. Using a sharp knife, make a shallow slit along the back of each prawn, then pull out the dark vein and discard. Rinse the prawns under cold water and dry well on kitchen paper.

2 Cut the chilli in half lengthways, remove the seeds and finely chop the flesh. It is important either to wear gloves while handling chillies or to wash your hands very thoroughly afterwards because their juices can cause irritation to sensitive skin, especially round the eyes, nose or mouth. Do not rub your eyes after touching the cut flesh of the chilli.

3 Heat the olive oil in a large, heavy-based frying pan or ovenproof casserole until quite hot, then add the garlic and cook for 30 seconds. Add the prawns, chilli, paprika and a pinch of salt and cook for 2–3 minutes, stirring all the time, until the prawns turn pink and start to curl.

4 Serve the prawns in the cooking dish, still sizzling. Accompany with cocktail sticks to spear the prawns and chunks or slices of crusty bread to mop up the cooking oil.

spicy prawns in sherry

ingredients

SERVES 4

12 raw Mediterranean prawns

2 tbsp olive oil

2 tbsp dry sherry

pinch of cayenne pepper or
    dash of Tabasco sauce

salt and pepper

method

1 Pull the heads off the prawns and peel, leaving the tails intact. Cut along the length of the back of each prawn and remove and discard the dark vein. Rinse and pat dry.

2 Heat the olive oil in a large, heavy-based frying pan. Add the prawns and cook over medium heat, stirring occasionally, for 2–3 minutes or until they have turned pink. Add the sherry and season to taste with cayenne, salt and pepper.

3 Tip the contents of the frying pan onto a serving platter. Impale each prawn with a wooden cocktail stick and serve.

crab tartlets

ingredients

MAKES 24

1 tbsp Spanish olive oil

1 small onion, finely chopped

1 garlic clove, finely chopped

splash of dry white wine

2 eggs

150 ml/5 fl oz milk or single
    cream

175 g/6 oz canned crabmeat,
    drained

55 g/2 oz Manchego or
    Parmesan cheese, grated

2 tbsp chopped fresh
    flat-leaf parsley

pinch of freshly grated nutmeg

salt and pepper

sprigs of fresh dill, to garnish

pastry

300 g/12 oz plain flour, plus
    extra for dusting

pinch of salt

175 g/6 oz butter

2 tbsp cold water

method

1 To prepare the crabmeat filling, heat the olive oil in a heavy-based frying pan, add the onion and cook for 5 minutes or until softened but not browned. Add the garlic and cook for an additional 30 seconds. Add a splash of wine and cook for 1–2 minutes or until most of the wine has evaporated.

2 Lightly whisk the eggs in a large mixing bowl, then whisk in the milk or cream. Add the crabmeat, cheese, parsley and the onion mixture. Season with nutmeg, salt and pepper and mix well together.

3 To prepare the pastry, mix the flour and salt together in a large mixing bowl. Add the butter, cut into small pieces and rub in until the mixture resembles fine breadcrumbs. Gradually stir in enough of the water to form a firm dough.

4 On a lightly floured work surface, thinly roll out the pastry. Using a plain, round 7-cm/2³/₄-inch cutter, cut out 24 circles. Use to line 24 x 4-cm/1¹/₂-inch tartlet tins. Carefully spoon the crabmeat mixture into the pastry cases, taking care not to overfill them. Bake in a preheated oven, 190°C/375°F, for 25–30 minutes or until golden brown and set. Serve the crab tartlets hot or cold, garnished with fresh dill sprigs.

spanish spinach & tomato pizzas

ingredients

MAKES 32

2 tbsp Spanish olive oil,
    plus extra for brushing
    and drizzling
1 onion, finely chopped
1 garlic clove, finely chopped
400 g/14 oz canned
    chopped tomatoes
125 g/4^1/$_2$ oz baby spinach
    leaves
salt and pepper
2 tbsp pine nuts

bread dough

4 tbsp warm water
^{1}/$_2$ tsp active dry yeast
pinch of sugar
220 g/7 oz white bread flour,
    plus extra for dusting
^{1}/$_2$ tsp salt

method

1 To make the bread dough, measure the water into a small bowl, sprinkle in the dry yeast and sugar and allow to stand in a warm place for 10–15 minutes or until frothy.

2 Sift the flour and salt into a large bowl. Make a well in the centre, pour in the yeast, then stir together. Work the dough with your hands until it leaves the sides of the bowl clean. Turn out onto a lightly floured work surface and knead for 10 minutes or until smooth and elastic. Put in a clean bowl, cover with a damp tea towel and stand in a warm place for 1 hour or until risen and doubled in size.

3 To make the topping, heat the olive oil in a large frying pan. Cook the onion until softened but not browned. Add the garlic and cook for 30 seconds. Stir in the tomatoes and cook until reduced to a thick sauce. Stir in the spinach leaves until wilted. Season to taste.

4 Turn the risen dough out and knead well for 2–3 minutes. Roll out very thinly and, using a 6-cm/2^1/$_2$-inch plain round cutter, cut out 32 circles. Place on baking sheets brushed with olive oil. Cover each base with the spinach mixture. Sprinkle with pine nuts and drizzle over a little olive oil. Bake in a preheated oven, 200°C/400°F, for 10–15 minutes or until the edges of the dough are golden. Serve hot.

stuffed cherry tomatoes

ingredients

SERVES 8

24 cherry tomatoes

anchovy and olive filling

50 g/1³/₄ oz canned
    anchovies in olive oil
8 pimiento-stuffed green
    olives, finely chopped
2 large hard-boiled eggs,
    finely chopped
pepper

crab salad filling

175 g/6 oz canned crabmeat,
    drained
4 tbsp mayonnaise
1 tbsp chopped fresh
    flat-leaf parsley
salt and pepper

black olive and caper filling

12 pitted black olives
3 tbsp capers
6 tbsp aïoli (see page 70)
salt and pepper

method

1 If necessary, cut and discard a very thin slice from the stalk end of each tomato to make the bases flat and stable. Cut a thin slice from the smooth end of each tomato and discard. Using a serrated knife or teaspoon, scoop out and discard the pulp and seeds. Turn the tomatoes upside down on kitchen paper and allow to drain for 5 minutes.

2 To make the anchovy and olive filling, drain the anchovies, reserving the oil for later, chop finely and put in a bowl. Add the olives and hard-boiled eggs. Pour in a trickle of oil from the drained anchovies to moisten the mixture, season with pepper (the anchovies will provide enough salt) and mix well together.

3 To make the crab salad filling, put the crabmeat, mayonnaise and parsley in a bowl and mix well together. Season the filling to taste with salt and pepper.

4 To make the black olive and caper filling, put the olives and capers on kitchen paper to drain them well, then chop finely and put in a bowl. Add the aïoli and mix well together. Season the filling to taste with salt and pepper.

5 Fill a piping bag fitted with a 2-cm/³/₄-inch plain tip with the filling of your choice and use to pack the filling into the hollow tomato shells. Store the tomatoes in the refrigerator until ready to serve.

sautéed garlic mushrooms

ingredients

SERVES 6

450 g/1 lb white mushrooms

5 tbsp Spanish olive oil

2 garlic cloves, finely chopped

squeeze of lemon juice

salt and pepper

4 tbsp chopped fresh
   flat-leaf parsley

crusty bread, to serve

method

1 Wipe or brush clean the mushrooms, then trim off the stalks close to the caps. Cut any large mushrooms in half or into quarters. Heat the olive oil in a large, heavy-based frying pan, add the garlic and cook for 30 seconds– 1 minute or until lightly browned. Add the mushrooms and sauté over high heat, stirring most of the time, until the mushrooms have absorbed all the oil in the frying pan.

2 Reduce the heat to low. When the juices have come out of the mushrooms, increase the heat again and sauté for 4–5 minutes, stirring most of the time, until the juices have almost evaporated. Add a squeeze of lemon juice and season to taste with salt and pepper. Stir in the chopped parsley and cook for an additional minute.

3 Transfer the sautéed mushrooms to a warmed serving dish and serve piping hot or warm. Accompany with chunks or slices of crusty bread for mopping up the garlic cooking juices.

chilli mushrooms

ingredients

SERVES 6–8

55 g/2 oz butter

5 tbsp olive oil

1 kg/2 lb 4 oz white mushrooms

4 fat garlic cloves,
    finely chopped

1 fresh red chilli, deseeded
    and finely chopped

1 tbsp lemon juice

salt and pepper

fresh parsley sprigs,
    to garnish

method

1 Heat the butter with the olive oil in a large, heavy-based frying pan. When the butter has melted, add the mushrooms, garlic and chilli and cook over medium–low heat, stirring frequently, for 5 minutes.

2 Stir in the lemon juice and season the mushrooms to taste with salt and pepper.

3 Transfer to warmed serving dishes and serve immediately, garnished with parsley sprigs.

deep-fried cauliflower

ingredients

SERVES 4–6

1 cauliflower, cut into florets

1 egg

150 ml/5 fl oz milk

115 g/4 oz plain flour

salt

vegetable oil, for deep-frying

tomato & pepper salsa
(see below), or aïoli
(see page 70), to serve

pepper and tomato salsa

4 tbsp olive oil

10 large garlic cloves

140 g/5 oz spring onions,
chopped

4 large red peppers,
deseeded and chopped

1 kg/2 lb 4 oz ripe, fresh
tomatoes, chopped

2 thin strips freshly pared
orange rind

pinch of hot red pepper
flakes, to taste (optional)

salt and pepper

method

1 To make the salsa, heat the olive oil in a large, flameproof casserole dish over medium heat. Add the garlic, spring onions and peppers and cook for 10 minutes, stirring occasionally, until the peppers are soft but not brown. Add the tomatoes, orange rind, hot pepper flakes, if using, and salt and pepper to taste and bring to the boil. Reduce the heat to as low as possible and allow to simmer, uncovered, for 45 minutes or until the liquid evaporates and the sauce thickens. Purée the sauce in a food processor then press through a fine sieve.

2 Bring a large saucepan of lightly salted water to the boil. Add the cauliflower florets, then reduce the heat and simmer gently for 5 minutes. Drain well, then refresh under cold running water and drain again.

3 Beat the egg and milk together in a bowl until combined. Gradually whisk in the flour and 1 teaspoon salt.

4 Meanwhile, heat the vegetable oil for deep-frying to 180–190°C/350–375°F, or until a cube of bread browns in 30 seconds.

5 Dip the cauliflower florets in the batter and drain off the excess, then deep-fry, in batches if necessary, for 5 minutes or until golden. Drain on kitchen paper, then serve at once in warmed bowls with the salsa or aïoli.

made with vegetables

Many tapas dishes are based on vegetables, which in Spain are treated with great respect and loving care. The Spanish serve tapas vegetable dishes when the vegetables are in season and, for authenticity, you should do the same where possible. However, some of the recipes in this chapter do 'cheat' and use vegetables preserved in oil, such as pimientos and artichoke hearts, which are readily available and quite excellent, as well as time-saving.

Potato dishes are particularly popular tapas, and those using baby new potatoes are a great way to take advantage when these are in season locally. They go very well with aïoli, a rich, garlic mayonnaise from Catalonia. It is well worth acquiring the art of making this delectable sauce from scratch, because it is a tapas classic and appears on every tapas menu. Potato-based tapas dishes can be served as bite-size nibbles on cocktail sticks, or as side dishes with some of the other tasty recipes in this chapter that use everything from colourful peppers, aubergines and tomatoes – all of which are very good roasted – to green beans and broad beans, served in a dressing. Other vegetable dishes are made substantial by the addition of a stuffing – rice is particularly suitable for this. Eating vegetables has never looked so good!

roasted pepper salad

ingredients

SERVES 8

3 red peppers

3 yellow peppers

5 tbsp Spanish extra-virgin
   olive oil

2 tbsp dry sherry vinegar or
   lemon juice

2 garlic cloves, crushed

pinch of sugar

salt and pepper

1 tbsp capers

8 small black Spanish olives

2 tbsp chopped fresh
   marjoram, plus extra
   sprigs to garnish

method

1 Preheat the grill to high. Place the peppers on a wire rack or grill pan and cook under the grill for 10 minutes or until their skins have blackened and blistered, turning them frequently.

2 Remove the roasted peppers from the heat and either put them in a bowl and immediately cover tightly with a clean, damp tea towel or put them in a plastic bag. The steam helps to soften the skins and makes it easier to remove them. Set them aside for about 15 minutes or until they are cool enough to handle.

3 Holding one pepper at a time over a clean bowl, use a sharp knife to make a small hole in the base and gently squeeze out the juices and reserve them. Still holding the pepper over the bowl, carefully peel off the blackened skin with your fingers or a knife and discard it. Cut the peppers in half and remove the stem, core and seeds, then cut each pepper into neat thin strips. Arrange the pepper strips on a serving dish.

4 To the reserved pepper juices add the olive oil, sherry vinegar, garlic, sugar, salt and pepper. Whisk together until combined. Drizzle the dressing evenly over the salad.

5 Sprinkle the capers, olives and chopped marjoram over the salad, garnish with marjoram sprigs and serve at room temperature.

red peppers with vinegar & capers

ingredients

SERVES 6

1 tbsp capers

4 tbsp olive oil

1 kg/2 lb 4 oz red peppers,
    halved, deseeded and cut
    into strips

4 garlic cloves, finely
    chopped

2 tbsp sherry vinegar

salt and pepper

method

1 If using salted capers, brush off most of the salt with your fingers. If using pickled capers in vinegar, drain well and rinse thoroughly.

2 Heat the oil in a heavy-based frying pan. Add the pepper strips and cook over medium heat, stirring frequently, for 10 minutes or until softened and charred around the edges. Add the capers and garlic and cook for an additional 2–3 minutes.

3 Stir in the vinegar and season to taste with salt and pepper – season sparingly with salt if using salted capers. Cook for 1–2 minutes, then remove from the heat. Serve immediately or set aside to cool, then cover and chill before serving.

roasted peppers with honey & almonds

ingredients

SERVES 6

8 red peppers, cut into
    quarters and deseeded

4 tbsp olive oil

2 garlic cloves, thinly sliced

25 g/1 oz flaked almonds

2 tbsp clear honey

2 tbsp sherry vinegar

2 tbsp chopped fresh parsley

salt and pepper

method

1 Preheat the grill to high. Place the peppers, skin-side up, in a single layer on a baking sheet. Cook under the hot grill for 8–10 minutes or until the skins have blistered and blackened. Using tongs, transfer to a plastic bag. Tie the top and set aside to cool.

2 When the peppers are cool enough to handle, peel off the skin with your fingers or a knife and discard it. Chop the flesh into bite-size pieces and place in a bowl.

3 Heat the olive oil in a large, heavy-based frying pan. Add the garlic and cook over low heat, stirring frequently, for 4 minutes or until golden. Stir in the almonds, honey and vinegar, then pour the mixture over the pepper pieces. Add the parsley and season to taste with salt and pepper, then toss well.

4 Allow to cool to room temperature, then transfer to serving dishes. The peppers may also be covered and stored in the refrigerator but should be returned to room temperature to serve.

stuffed pimientos

ingredients

SERVES 7–8

185 g/6$^{1/2}$ oz bottled whole
    pimientos del piquillo

fillings
curd cheese
and herb

225 g/8 oz curd cheese

1 tsp lemon juice

1 garlic clove, crushed

4 tbsp chopped fresh
    flat-leaf parsley

1 tbsp chopped fresh mint

1 tbsp chopped
    fresh oregano

salt and pepper

tuna mayonnaise

200 g/7 oz canned tuna steak
    in olive oil, drained

5 tbsp mayonnaise

2 tsp lemon juice

2 tbsp chopped fresh
    flat-leaf parsley

salt and pepper

goat's cheese
and olive

50 g/1$^{3/4}$ oz pitted black
    olives, finely chopped

200 g/7 oz soft goat's cheese

1 garlic clove, crushed

salt and pepper

method

1 Lift the pimientos from the jar, reserving the oil for later.

2 To make the curd cheese and herb filling, put the curd cheese in a bowl and add the lemon juice, garlic, parsley, mint and oregano. Mix well together. Season to taste with salt and pepper.

3 To make the tuna mayonnaise filling, put the tuna in a bowl and add the mayonnaise, lemon juice and parsley. Add 1 tablespoon of the reserved oil from the jar of pimientos and mix well. Season to taste with salt and pepper.

4 To make the goat's cheese and olive filling, put the olives in a bowl and add the goat's cheese, garlic and 1 tablespoon of the reserved oil from the jar of pimientos. Mix well together. Season to taste with salt and pepper.

5 Using a teaspoon, heap the filling of your choice into each pimiento. Put in the refrigerator and chill for at least 2 hours until firm.

6 To serve the pimientos, arrange them on a serving plate and, if necessary, wipe with kitchen paper to remove any of the filling that has spread over the skins.

stuffed peppers

ingredients

MAKES 6

6 tbsp olive oil, plus a little
   extra for rubbing on
   peppers

2 onions, finely chopped

2 garlic cloves, crushed

140 g/5 oz Spanish short-
   grain rice

55 g/2 oz raisins

55 g/2 oz pine nuts

40 g/1$\frac{1}{2}$ oz fresh parsley,
   finely chopped

salt and pepper

1 tbsp tomato purée dissolved
   in 750 ml/1$\frac{1}{4}$ pints
   hot water

4–6 red, green or yellow
   peppers (or a mix of
   colours), or 6 of the long,
   Mediterranean variety

method

1 Preheat the oven to 200°C/400°F. Heat the oil in a shallow, heavy-based flameproof casserole dish. Add the onions and cook for 3 minutes. Add the garlic and cook for an additional 2 minutes or until the onion is soft but not brown.

2 Stir in the rice, raisins and pine nuts until all are coated in the oil, then add half the parsley and salt and pepper to taste. Stir in the tomato purée and bring to the boil. Reduce the heat and simmer, uncovered, shaking the casserole dish frequently, for 20 minutes or until the rice is tender, the liquid is absorbed and small holes appear on the surface. Watch carefully because the raisins can catch and burn. Stir in the remaining parsley, then cool slightly.

3 While the rice is simmering, cut the top off each pepper and reserve. Remove the core and seeds from each pepper.

4 Divide the stuffing equally between the peppers. Use wooden cocktail sticks to secure the tops back in place. Lightly rub each pepper with olive oil and arrange in a single layer in an ovenproof dish. Bake in the preheated oven for 30 minutes or until the peppers are tender. Serve hot or cool to room temperature.

baby potatoes with aïoli

ingredients

SERVES 6–8

450 g/1 lb baby new potatoes
1 tbsp chopped fresh
    flat-leaf parsley
salt

aïoli

1 large egg yolk, at room
    temperature
1 tbsp white wine vinegar or
    lemon juice
2 large garlic cloves, peeled
salt and pepper
5 tbsp Spanish extra-virgin
    olive oil
5 tbsp corn oil

method

1 To make the aïoli, blend the egg yolk, vinegar, garlic, salt and pepper in a food processor. With the motor still running, very slowly add the olive oil, then the corn oil, drop by drop at first, then, when it starts to thicken, in a slow steady stream until the sauce is thick and smooth. Alternatively, mix in a bowl with a whisk.

2 For this recipe, the aïoli should be a little thin so that it coats the potatoes. To ensure this, quickly blend in 1 tablespoon water so that it forms the consistency of sauce.

3 To prepare the potatoes, cut them in half or quarters to make bite-size pieces. If they are very small, you can leave them whole. Put the potatoes in a large saucepan of cold, salted water and bring to the boil. Lower the heat and simmer for 7 minutes or until just tender. Drain well, then turn out into a large bowl.

4 While the potatoes are still warm, pour over the aïoli sauce and gently toss the potatoes in it. Adding the sauce to the potatoes while they are still warm will help them to absorb the garlic flavour. Set aside for about 20 minutes to allow the potatoes to marinate in the sauce.

5 Transfer the potatoes with aïoli to a warmed serving dish, sprinkle over the parsley and salt and serve warm. Alternatively, the aïoli can be served separately, allowing diners to dip the potatoes themselves.

pan-fried potatoes with piquant paprika

ingredients

SERVES 6

3 tsp paprika

1 tsp ground cumin

$1/4$–$1/2$ tsp cayenne pepper

$1/2$ tsp salt

450 g/1 lb small old potatoes, peeled

corn oil, for pan-frying

sprigs of fresh flat-leaf parsley, to garnish

aïoli, to serve (see page 70) (optional)

method

1 Put the paprika, cumin, cayenne pepper and salt in a small bowl and mix well together. Set aside.

2 Cut each potato into 8 thick wedges. Pour corn oil into a large, heavy-based frying pan to a depth of about 2.5 cm/1 inch. Heat the oil, then add the potato wedges, preferably in a single layer and cook gently for 10 minutes or until golden brown all over, turning from time to time. Remove from the frying pan with a slotted spoon and drain on kitchen paper.

3 Transfer the potato wedges to a large bowl and, while they are still hot, sprinkle with the paprika mixture, then gently toss them together to coat.

4 Turn the potatoes into a large, warmed serving dish, several smaller ones or onto individual plates and serve hot, garnished with parsley sprigs. Accompany with a bowl of aïoli for dipping, if wished.

spanish potatoes

ingredients

SERVES 4

2 tbsp olive oil

500 g/1 lb 2 oz small new
   potatoes, halved

1 onion, halved and sliced

1 green pepper, deseeded
   and cut into strips

1 tsp chilli powder

1 tsp mustard

300 ml/10 fl oz canned
   tomatoes, sieved

300 ml/10 fl oz vegetable
   stock

salt and pepper

chopped fresh parsley,
   to garnish

method

1 Heat the olive oil in a large, heavy-based frying pan. Add the potatoes and onion and cook, stirring frequently, for 4–5 minutes or until the onions are soft and translucent.

2 Add the pepper strips, chilli powder and mustard to the pan and cook for 2–3 minutes.

3 Stir the sieved tomatoes and vegetable stock into the pan and bring to the boil. Reduce the heat and simmer for 25 minutes or until the potatoes are tender. Season to taste with salt and pepper.

4 Transfer the potatoes to a warmed serving dish. Sprinkle the chopped parsley over the top and serve immediately. Alternatively, set the potatoes aside to cool completely and serve at room temperature.

feisty potatoes

ingredients

SERVES 6

1 kg/2 lb 4 oz potatoes,
    unpeeled

olive oil

sea salt

aïoli (see page 70), to serve

chilli oil

150 ml/5 fl oz olive oil

2 small hot fresh red chillies,
    slit

1 tsp hot Spanish paprika

method

1 To make the chilli oil, heat the olive oil and chillies over high heat until the chillies begin to sizzle. Remove the saucepan from the heat and stir in the paprika. Set aside to cool, then transfer the chilli oil to a pourer with a spout. Do not strain.

2 Scrub the potatoes, pat them dry and cut into chunky pieces. Put 1 cm/$1/2$ inch olive oil and one potato piece in one or each of two large, heavy-based frying pans over medium–high heat and heat until the potato begins to sizzle. Add the remaining potatoes without crowding the pans and fry for 15 minutes or until golden brown all over and tender. Work in batches, if necessary, keeping the cooked potatoes warm while you fry the remainder. Use a slotted spoon to transfer the potatoes to a plate covered with crumpled kitchen paper.

3 To serve, divide the potatoes between 6 serving plates and add a serving of aïoli to each. Drizzle with chilli oil and serve either warm or at room temperature.

warm potato salad

ingredients

SERVES 4–6

175 ml/6 fl oz olive oil

450 g/1 lb waxy potatoes,
    thinly sliced

salt and pepper

50 ml/2 fl oz white wine
    vinegar

2 garlic cloves, finely
    chopped

method

1 Heat 50 ml/2 fl oz of the olive oil in a large, heavy-based frying pan. Add the potato slices and season to taste with salt, then cook over low heat, shaking the frying pan occasionally, for 10 minutes. Turn the potatoes over and cook for an additional 5 minutes or until tender but not browned.

2 Meanwhile, pour the vinegar into a small saucepan. Add the garlic and season to taste with pepper. Bring to the boil, then stir in the remaining olive oil.

3 Transfer the potatoes to a bowl and pour over the dressing. Toss gently and set aside for 15 minutes. Using a slotted spoon, transfer the potatoes to individual serving dishes and serve warm.

broad beans with cheese & prawns

ingredients

SERVES 6

500 g/1 lb 2 oz shelled fresh
   or frozen broad beans

2 fresh thyme sprigs

225 g/8 oz cooked, peeled
   prawns

225 g/8 oz Queso Majorero or
   Gruyère cheese, diced

6 tbsp olive oil

2 tbsp lemon juice

1 garlic clove, finely chopped

salt and pepper

method

1 Bring a large saucepan of lightly salted water to the boil. Add the broad beans and 1 thyme sprig, then reduce the heat and simmer, covered, for 7 minutes. Drain well and refresh under cold running water, then drain again.

2 Unless the broad beans are very young, remove and discard the outer skins. Place the beans in a bowl and add the prawns and cheese.

3 Chop the remaining thyme sprig. Whisk the olive oil, lemon juice, garlic and chopped thyme together in a separate bowl and season to taste with salt and pepper.

4 Pour the dressing over the bean mixture. Toss lightly and serve.

green beans with pine nuts

ingredients

SERVES 8

2 tbsp Spanish olive oil

50 g/1³/₄ oz pine nuts

¹/₂–1 tsp paprika

450 g/1 lb green beans

1 small onion, finely chopped

1 garlic clove, finely chopped

salt and pepper

juice of ¹/₂ lemon

method

1 Heat the oil in a large, heavy-based frying pan, add the pine nuts and cook for about 1 minute, stirring all the time and shaking the frying pan, until light golden brown. Using a slotted spoon, remove the pine nuts from the frying pan, drain well on kitchen paper, then transfer to a bowl. Set aside the oil in the frying pan for later. Add the paprika, according to taste, to the pine nuts, stir together until coated and then set aside.

2 Trim the green beans and remove any strings if necessary. Put the beans in a saucepan, pour over boiling water, return to the boil and cook for 5 minutes or until tender but still firm. Drain well in a sieve.

3 Reheat the oil in the frying pan, add the onion and cook for 5–10 minutes or until softened and starting to brown. Add the garlic and cook for an additional 30 seconds.

4 Add the beans to the frying pan and cook for 2–3 minutes, tossing together with the onion until heated through. Season the beans to taste with salt and pepper.

5 Turn the contents of the frying pan into a warmed serving dish, sprinkle over the lemon juice and toss together. Sprinkle over the golden pine nuts and serve hot.

mixed beans

ingredients

SERVES 4–6

175 g/6 oz shelled fresh or
  frozen broad beans
115 g/4 oz fresh or frozen
  green beans
115 g/4 oz mangetout
1 shallot, finely chopped
6 fresh mint sprigs
4 tbsp olive oil
1 tbsp sherry vinegar
1 garlic clove, finely chopped
salt and pepper

method

1 Bring a large saucepan of lightly salted water to the boil. Add the broad beans and reduce the heat, then cover and simmer for 7 minutes. Remove the beans with a slotted spoon, then plunge into cold water and drain. Remove and discard the outer skins.

2 Meanwhile, return the saucepan of salted water to the boil. Add the green beans and mangetout and return to the boil again. Drain and refresh under cold running water. Drain well.

3 Mix the broad beans, green beans, mangetout and shallot together in a bowl. Strip the leaves from the mint sprigs, then reserve half and add the remainder to the bean mixture. Finely chop the reserved mint.

4 Whisk the olive oil, vinegar, garlic and chopped mint together in a separate bowl and season to taste with salt and pepper. Pour the dressing over the bean mixture and toss lightly to coat. Cover with clingfilm and chill until required.

white bean vinaigrette

ingredients

SERVES 4–6

400 g/14 oz canned white
   beans

3 celery stalks, chopped

1 gherkin, finely chopped

150 ml/5 fl oz olive oil

4 tbsp white wine vinegar

1 garlic clove, finely chopped

2 tsp Dijon mustard

1 tbsp chopped fresh parsley

pinch of sugar

salt and pepper

snipped fresh chives,
   to garnish

method

1 Drain the beans and rinse well under cold running water, then drain again. Place the beans, celery and gherkin in a bowl.

2 Whisk the olive oil, vinegar, garlic, mustard, parsley and sugar together in a bowl and season to taste with salt and pepper.

3 Pour the vinaigrette over the bean mixture and toss well. Transfer to a serving dish and sprinkle with the snipped chives, then serve at room temperature or cover and chill before serving.

garlic tomatoes

ingredients

SERVES 6

8 deep red tomatoes

3 fresh thyme sprigs, plus
    extra to garnish

12 garlic cloves, unpeeled

75 ml/2$\frac{1}{2}$ fl oz olive oil

salt and pepper

method

1 Preheat the oven to 220°C/425°F. Cut the tomatoes in half lengthways and arrange, cut-side up, in a single layer in a large, ovenproof dish. Tuck the thyme sprigs and garlic cloves between them.

2 Drizzle the olive oil all over the tomatoes and season to taste with pepper. Bake in the preheated oven for 40–45 minutes or until the tomatoes are softened and beginning to char slightly around the edges.

3 Remove and discard the thyme sprigs. Season the tomatoes to taste with salt and pepper. Garnish with the extra thyme sprigs and serve hot or warm. Squeeze the pulp from the garlic over the tomatoes at the table.

baked tomato nests

ingredients

SERVES 4

4 large ripe tomatoes

salt and pepper

4 large eggs

4 tbsp double cream

4 tbsp grated mature Mahon,
    Manchego or Parmesan
    cheese

method

1 Preheat the oven to 180°C/350°F. Cut a slice off the tops of the tomatoes and, using a teaspoon, carefully scoop out the pulp and seeds without piercing the shells. Turn the tomato shells upside down on kitchen paper and drain for 15 minutes. Season the insides of the shells with salt and pepper.

2 Place the tomatoes in an ovenproof dish just large enough to hold them in a single layer. Carefully break 1 egg into each tomato shell, then top with 1 tablespoon of cream and 1 tablespoon of grated cheese.

3 Bake in the preheated oven for 15–20 minutes or until the eggs are just set. Serve hot.

stuffed tomatoes with rice

ingredients

SERVES 4–8

140 g/5 oz long-grain rice

140 g/5 oz black olives, pitted
    and chopped

3 tbsp olive oil

salt and pepper

4 beefsteak or other large
    tomatoes, halved

4 tbsp chopped fresh parsley

method

1 Bring a large saucepan of lightly salted water to the boil. Add the rice, then return to the boil and stir once. Reduce the heat and cook for 10–15 minutes or until only just tender. Drain well, then rinse under cold running water and drain again. Line a large, shallow dish with kitchen paper and spread out the rice on top for about 1 hour to dry.

2 Mix the rice, olives and olive oil together in a bowl and season well with pepper. You will probably not require any additional salt. Cover with clingfilm and stand at room temperature for 8 hours or overnight.

3 Cut a slice off the tops of the tomatoes and, using a teaspoon, carefully scoop out and discard the seeds without piercing the shells. Scoop out the flesh, then finely chop and add to the rice and olive mixture. Season the insides of the shells to taste with salt, then turn them upside down on kitchen paper and drain for 1 hour.

4 Pat the insides of the tomato shells dry with kitchen paper, then divide the rice and olive mixture between them. Sprinkle with the parsley and serve.

artichoke hearts & asparagus

ingredients

SERVES 4–6

450 g/1 lb asparagus spears

400 g/14 oz canned artichoke hearts, drained and rinsed

2 tbsp freshly squeezed orange juice

1/2 tsp finely grated orange rind

2 tbsp walnut oil

1 tsp Dijon mustard

salt and pepper

salad leaves, to serve

method

1 Trim and discard the coarse, woody ends of the asparagus spears. Make sure all the stems are about the same length, then tie them together loosely with clean kitchen string. If you have an asparagus steamer, you don't need to tie the stems together – just place them in the basket.

2 Bring a tall saucepan of lightly salted water to the boil. Add the asparagus, making sure that the tips are protruding above the water, then reduce the heat and simmer for 10–15 minutes or until tender. Test by piercing a stem just above the water level with the point of a sharp knife. Drain, then refresh under cold running water and drain again.

3 Cut the asparagus spears into 2.5-cm/1-inch pieces, keeping the tips intact. Cut the artichoke hearts into small wedges and combine with the asparagus in a bowl.

4 Whisk the orange juice, orange rind, walnut oil and mustard together in a bowl and season to taste with salt and pepper. If serving immediately, pour the dressing over the artichoke hearts and asparagus and toss lightly.

5 Arrange the salad leaves in individual serving dishes and top with the artichoke and asparagus mixture. Serve immediately.

artichoke hearts and peas

ingredients

SERVES 4–6

4 tbsp extra-virgin olive oil

2 onions, sliced finely

1 large garlic clove, crushed

280 g/10 oz artichoke hearts
preserved in oil, drained
and halved

200 g/7 oz frozen or fresh
shelled peas

2 red peppers, grilled,
deseeded and sliced

2 thin slices serrano ham
or prosciutto, chopped

6 tbsp finely chopped fresh
parsley

juice 1/2 lemon

salt and pepper

method

1 Heat the oil in a flameproof casserole dish over medium–high heat. Add the onions and cook, stirring, for 3 minutes, then add the garlic and cook for 2 minutes or until the onions are soft but not brown.

2 Add the halved artichoke hearts and fresh peas, if using, along with just enough water to cover. Bring to the boil, then reduce the heat and simmer, uncovered, for 5 minutes or until the peas are cooked through and all the water has evaporated.

3 Stir in the peppers, ham or prosciutto and frozen peas, if using. Continue simmering just long enough to warm through. Stir in the parsley and lemon juice to taste. Add salt and pepper, remembering that the ham is salty. Serve at once or cool to room temperature.

stuffed mushrooms

ingredients

SERVES 6

175 g/6 oz butter

4 garlic cloves, finely chopped

6 large open mushrooms,
   stems removed

55 g/2 oz fresh white
   breadcrumbs

1 tbsp chopped fresh thyme

salt and pepper

1 egg, lightly beaten

method

1 Preheat the oven to 180°C/350°F. Cream the butter in a bowl until softened, then beat in the garlic. Divide two-thirds of the garlic butter between the mushroom caps and arrange them, cup-side up, on a baking sheet.

2 Melt the remaining garlic butter in a heavy-based or non-stick frying pan. Add the breadcrumbs and cook over low heat, stirring frequently, until golden. Remove from the heat and tip into a bowl. Stir in the thyme and season to taste with salt and pepper. Stir in the beaten egg until thoroughly combined.

3 Divide the breadcrumb mixture between the mushroom caps and bake in the preheated oven for 15 minutes or until the stuffing is golden brown and the mushrooms are tender. Serve hot or warm.

marinated aubergines

ingredients

SERVES 4

2 aubergines, halved
    lengthways
salt and pepper
4 tbsp olive oil
2 garlic cloves,
    finely chopped
2 tbsp chopped fresh parsley
1 tbsp chopped fresh thyme
2 tbsp lemon juice

method

1 Make 3 slashes in the flesh of the aubergine halves and place, cut-side down, in an ovenproof dish. Season to taste with salt and pepper, then pour over the olive oil and sprinkle with the garlic, parsley and thyme. Cover and marinate at room temperature for 2–3 hours.

2 Preheat the oven to 180°C/350°F. Uncover the dish and roast the aubergines in the preheated oven for 45 minutes. Remove the dish from the oven and turn the aubergines over. Baste with the cooking juices and sprinkle with the lemon juice. Return to the oven and cook for an additional 15 minutes.

3 Transfer the aubergines to serving plates. Spoon over the cooking juices and serve hot or warm.

chargrilled leeks

ingredients

SERVES 4

8 baby leeks

2 tbsp olive oil, plus extra
   for brushing

2 tbsp white wine vinegar

2 tbsp snipped fresh chives

2 tbsp chopped fresh parsley

1 tsp Dijon mustard

salt and pepper

fresh parsley sprigs,
   to garnish

method

1 Trim the leeks and halve lengthways. Rinse thoroughly to remove any grit and pat dry with kitchen paper.

2 Heat a griddle pan and brush with olive oil. Add the leeks and cook over medium–high heat, turning occasionally, for 5 minutes. Transfer to a shallow dish.

3 Meanwhile, whisk the olive oil, vinegar, chives, parsley and mustard together in a bowl and season to taste with salt and pepper. Pour over the leeks, turning to coat. Cover with clingfilm and marinate at room temperature, turning occasionally, for 30 minutes.

4 Divide the leeks between individual serving plates, then garnish with parsley sprigs and serve.

orange & fennel salad

ingredients

SERVES 4

4 large, juicy oranges

1 large fennel bulb, very
thinly sliced

1 mild white onion,
finely sliced

2 tbsp extra-virgin olive oil

12 plump black olives, pitted
and thinly sliced

1 fresh red chilli, deseeded
and very thinly sliced
(optional)

finely chopped fresh parsley

French bread, to serve

method

1 Finely grate the rind from the oranges into a bowl and reserve. Using a small, serrated knife, remove all the white pith from the oranges, working over a bowl to catch the juices. Cut the oranges horizontally into thin slices.

2 Toss the orange slices with the fennel and onion slices. Whisk the olive oil into the reserved orange juice, then spoon over the oranges. Sprinkle the olive slices over the top, add the chilli, if using, then sprinkle with the orange rind and parsley. Serve with slices of French bread.

tomato & olive salad

ingredients

SERVES 6

2 tbsp sherry or red wine
    vinegar

5 tbsp olive oil

1 garlic clove, finely chopped

1 tsp paprika

salt

4 tomatoes, peeled and diced

12 anchovy-stuffed or
    pimiento-stuffed olives

$1/2$ cucumber, peeled and
    diced

2 shallots, finely chopped

1 tbsp pickled capers in
    brine, drained

2–3 chicory heads, separated
    into leaves

method

1 First, make the dressing. Whisk the vinegar, olive oil, garlic and paprika together in a bowl. Season to taste with salt and reserve.

2 Place the tomatoes, olives, cucumber, shallots and capers in a separate bowl. Pour the dressing over and toss lightly.

3 Line 6 individual serving bowls with chicory leaves. Spoon an equal quantity of the salad into the centre of each and serve.

sweet onion salad

ingredients

SERVES 4–6

4 Spanish onions

2 tbsp chopped fresh parsley

115 g/4 oz black olives, pitted

salt and pepper

1 tbsp sherry vinegar

2 tbsp red wine vinegar

125 ml/4 fl oz olive oil

about 1 tbsp water

method

1 Bring a large saucepan of lightly salted water to the boil. Add the onions and simmer for 20 minutes or until tender. Drain and set aside until cool enough to handle.

2 Thickly slice the onions and place in a shallow dish. Sprinkle the parsley and olives over and season to taste with pepper.

3 Whisk the vinegars and olive oil together in a bowl, then whisk in enough of the water to make a creamy vinaigrette.

4 Pour the dressing over the onions and olives and serve at room temperature.

for meat lovers

Although meat has never been as plentiful in Spain as it is in other countries, it does have a place in the culinary repertoire and the recipes in this chapter include the usual pork, lamb, beef and chicken that are available elsewhere. Of these, pork and chicken are perhaps the most popular with the Spaniards, as are cured Serrano ham and chorizo, the country's favourite sausage, which is flavoured with paprika and garlic and can be eaten cold or pan-fried, baked or cooked in a sauce.

If possible, serve these meat tapas dishes in small, earthenware bowls, just as they are seen on every bar counter in Spain. This is not just for the sake of authenticity, although they certainly look attractive – but also because they retain the heat or cold well, so will keep your tapas dish at the correct temperature while you and your guests relax over a glass of something chilled.

Some of these meat tapas make perfect light lunch or supper dishes – serve them with a salad and some good fresh country bread to mop up the juices. Try serving meatballs this way and you'll have a taste of something delicious to eat and also of a little Spanish history, as meatballs have been a feature of Spanish cookery since as far back as the thirteenth century.

fried chorizo with herbs

ingredients

SERVES 6–8

700 g/1 lb 9 oz chorizo
    cooking sausage

2 tbsp olive oil

2 garlic cloves,
    finely chopped

4 tbsp chopped mixed
    fresh herbs

method

1 Using a sharp knife, cut the chorizo into 5-mm/$1/4$-inch thick slices. Heat a large, heavy-based frying pan. Add the chorizo slices, without any additional fat, and cook over medium heat, stirring frequently, for 5 minutes or until crisp and browned.

2 Remove the chorizo slices with a spatula or slotted spoon and drain well on kitchen paper. Drain the fat from the frying pan and wipe out with a pad of kitchen paper.

3 Heat the olive oil in the frying pan over medium–low heat. Add the chorizo slices, garlic and herbs and cook, stirring occasionally, until heated through. Serve immediately.

salad of melon, chorizo & artichokes

ingredients

SERVES 8

12 small globe artichokes

juice of ½ lemon

2 tbsp Spanish olive oil

1 small orange-fleshed
    melon, such as
    cantaloupe, halved,
    deseeded and cut into
    bite-size cubes

200 g/7 oz chorizo sausage,
    outer casing removed and
    cut into bite-size chunks

few sprigs of fresh tarragon or
    flat-leaf parsley, to garnish

dressing

3 tbsp Spanish extra-virgin
    olive oil

1 tbsp red wine vinegar

1 tsp prepared mustard

1 tbsp chopped
    fresh tarragon

salt and pepper

method

1 To prepare the artichokes, cut off the stalks. Break off the toughest outer leaves at the base until the tender inside leaves are visible. Cut the spiky tips off the leaves with a pair of scissors. Using a sharp knife, pare the dark green skin from the base and down the stem. Brush the cut surfaces of the artichokes with lemon juice as you prepare them, to prevent discoloration. Unless you are using very young artichokes, carefully remove the choke (the mass of silky hairs) by pulling it out with your fingers or scooping it out with a spoon. It is important to remove all the choke as the little barbs, if eaten, can irritate the throat. Cut the artichokes into quarters and brush them again with lemon juice.

2 Heat the olive oil in a large, heavy-based frying pan. Add the artichokes and cook, stirring frequently, for 5 minutes or until the leaves are golden brown. Transfer the artichokes to a large serving bowl and set aside to cool. Add the melon cubes and chorizo chunks to the cooled artichokes.

3 To make the dressing, whisk all the ingredients together in a small bowl. Just before serving, pour the dressing over the salad and toss together. Serve the salad garnished with tarragon or parsley sprigs.

chickpeas & chorizo

ingredients

SERVES 4–6

250 g/9 oz chorizo sausage in
1 piece, outer casing
removed

4 tbsp olive oil

1 onion, finely chopped

1 large garlic clove, crushed

400 g/14 oz canned
chickpeas, drained
and rinsed

6 pimientos del piquillo,
drained, patted dry,
and sliced

1 tbsp sherry vinegar,
or to taste

salt and pepper

finely chopped fresh parsley,
to garnish

crusty bread slices, to serve

method

1 Cut the chorizo into 1-cm/$1/2$-inch dice. Heat the oil in a heavy-based frying pan over medium heat, then add the onion and garlic. Cook, stirring occasionally, until the onion is softened but not browned. Stir in the chorizo and cook until heated through.

2 Tip the mixture into a bowl and stir in the chickpeas and pimientos. Splash with sherry vinegar and season to taste with salt and pepper. Serve hot or at room temperature, generously sprinkled with parsley, with plenty of crusty bread.

chorizo empanadillas

ingredients

MAKES 12

125 g/4^1/2 oz chorizo
    sausage, outer casing
    removed
plain flour, for dusting
250 g/9 oz ready-made puff
    pastry, thawed if frozen
beaten egg, to glaze
paprika, to garnish

method

1 Preheat the oven to 200°C/400°F. Cut the chorizo sausage into small dice measuring about 1 cm/^{1}/2 inch square.

2 On a lightly floured work surface, thinly roll out the puff pastry. Using a plain, round 8-cm/3^1/4-inch cutter, cut into circles. Gently pile the trimmings together, roll out again, then cut out additional circles to produce 12 in total. Put about a teaspoonful of the chopped chorizo onto each of the pastry circles.

3 Dampen the edges of the pastry with a little water, then fold one half over the other half to completely cover the chorizo. Seal the edges together with your fingers. Using the prongs of a fork, press against the edges to give a decorative finish and seal them further. With the tip of a sharp knife, make a small slit in the side of each pastry. You can store the pastries in the refrigerator at this stage until you are ready to bake them.

4 Place the pastries onto dampened baking sheets and brush each with a little beaten egg to glaze. Bake in the oven for 10–15 minutes or until golden brown and puffed. Using a small sieve, lightly dust the top of each empanadilla with a little paprika to garnish. Serve the chorizo empanadillas hot or warm.

chorizo & mushroom kebabs

ingredients

MAKES 25

2 tbsp olive oil

25 pieces chorizo
  sausage, each about
  1-cm/^{1}/$_2$-inch square
  (about 100 g/3^1/$_2$ oz)

25 white mushrooms, wiped
  and stems removed

1 green pepper, grilled,
  peeled and cut into
  5 squares

method

1 Heat the olive oil in a frying pan over medium heat. Add the chorizo pieces and cook for 20 seconds, stirring.

2 Add the mushrooms and continue cooking for a further 1–2 minutes until the mushrooms begin to brown and absorb the fat in the pan.

3 Thread a pepper square, a piece of chorizo and a mushroom onto a wooden cocktail stick. Continue until all the ingredients are used. Serve hot or at room temperature.

chorizo in red wine

ingredients

SERVES 6

200 g/7 oz chorizo sausage

200 ml/7 fl oz Spanish red
   wine

2 tbsp brandy (optional)

fresh flat-leaf parsley sprigs,
   to garnish

crusty bread, to serve

method

1 Before you begin, bear in mind that this dish is best if prepared the day before you are planning to serve it. Using a fork, prick the chorizo in 3 or 4 places and pour wine over. Place the chorizo and wine in a large saucepan. Bring the wine to the boil, then reduce the heat and simmer gently, covered, for 15–20 minutes. Transfer the chorizo and wine to a bowl or dish, cover and let the sausage marinate in the wine for 8 hours or overnight.

2 The next day, remove the chorizo from the bowl or dish and reserve the wine. Remove the outer casing from the chorizo and cut the sausage into 5-mm/1/4-inch slices. Place the slices in a large, heavy-based frying pan or flameproof serving dish.

3 If you are adding the brandy, pour it into a small saucepan and heat gently. Pour the brandy over the chorizo slices, then stand well back and set alight. When the flames have died down, shake the pan gently and add the reserved wine to the pan, then cook over high heat until almost all of the wine has evaporated.

4 Serve the chorizo in red wine piping hot, in the dish in which it was cooked, sprinkled with parsley to garnish. Accompany with chunks or slices of bread to mop up the juices and provide wooden cocktail sticks to spear the pieces of chorizo.

broad beans with serrano ham

ingredients

SERVES 6–8

55 g/2 oz serrano or
  prosciutto, pancetta or
  rindless smoked lean bacon
115 g/4 oz chorizo sausage,
  outer casing removed
4 tbsp Spanish olive oil
1 onion, finely chopped
2 garlic cloves, finely chopped
splash of dry white wine
450 g/1 lb frozen broad
  beans, thawed, or about
  1.3 kg/3 lb fresh broad
  beans in their pods,
  shelled to give 450 g/1 lb
1 tbsp chopped fresh mint or
  dill, plus extra to garnish
pinch of sugar
salt and pepper

method

1 Using a sharp knife, cut the ham, pancetta or bacon into small strips. Cut the chorizo into 2-cm/3/4-inch cubes. Heat the olive oil in a large, heavy-based frying pan or ovenproof dish that has a lid. Add the onion and cook for 5 minutes or until softened and starting to brown. If you are using pancetta or bacon, add it with the onion. Add the garlic and cook for 30 seconds.

2 Pour the wine into the pan, increase the heat and let it bubble to evaporate the alcohol, then lower the heat. Add the broad beans, ham, if using, and the chorizo and cook for 1–2 minutes, stirring all the time to coat in the oil.

3 Cover the frying pan and let the beans simmer very gently in the oil, stirring from time to time, for 10–15 minutes or until the beans are tender. It may be necessary to add a little water to the frying pan during cooking, so keep an eye on it and add a splash if the beans appear to become too dry. Stir in the mint or dill and sugar. Season the dish with salt and pepper but taste first as you may find that it does not need any salt.

4 Transfer the broad beans to a large, warmed serving dish, several smaller ones, or individual plates and serve piping hot, garnished with chopped mint or dill.

serrano ham with rocket

ingredients

SERVES 6

140 g/5 oz rocket, separated
    into leaves
4^1/$_2$ tbsp olive oil
1^1/$_2$ tbsp orange juice
salt and pepper
280 g/10 oz thinly sliced
    serrano ham

method

1 Place the rocket in a bowl and pour in the olive oil and orange juice. Season to taste with salt and pepper and toss well.

2 Arrange the slices of ham on individual serving plates, folding it into attractive shapes. Divide the rocket between the plates and serve immediately.

tiny spanish meatballs in almond sauce

ingredients

SERVES 6–8

55 g/2 oz white or brown
   bread, crusts removed

3 tbsp water

450 g/1 lb lean ground pork

1 large onion, finely chopped

1 garlic clove, crushed

2 tbsp chopped fresh flat-leaf
   parsley, plus extra to garnish

1 egg, beaten

freshly grated nutmeg

salt and pepper

flour, for coating

2 tbsp Spanish olive oil

squeeze of lemon juice

almond sauce

2 tbsp Spanish olive oil

25 g/1 oz white or brown
   bread, torn into pieces

115 g/4 oz blanched almonds

2 garlic cloves, finely
   chopped

150 ml/5 fl oz dry white wine

salt and pepper

425 ml/15 fl oz vegetable
   stock

method

1 To prepare the meatballs, put the bread in a bowl, add the water and soak for 5 minutes. Squeeze out the water and return the bread to the dried bowl. Add the pork, onion, garlic, parsley and egg, then season with grated nutmeg and a little salt and pepper. Knead well to form a smooth mixture.

2 Spread some flour on a plate. With floured hands, shape the meat mixture into about 30 equal-sized balls, then coat each meatball in flour. Heat the olive oil in a large, heavy-based frying pan and cook the meatballs, in batches, for 4–5 minutes or until browned all over. Remove from the pan and set aside.

3 To make the almond sauce, heat the olive oil in the frying pan. Add the bread and almonds and cook gently, stirring, until golden. Add the garlic and cook for 30 seconds, then add the wine and boil for 1–2 minutes. Season to taste and let cool. Whiz in a food processor with the stock until smooth. Return to the pan.

4 Carefully add the meatballs to the sauce and simmer for 25 minutes or until the meatballs are tender. Transfer the meatballs and almond sauce to a serving dish, then add a squeeze of lemon juice to taste. Sprinkle with chopped parsley to garnish and serve with crusty bread.

tiny meatballs
with tomato sauce

ingredients

MAKES 60

olive oil

1 red onion, very finely chopped

500 g/1 lb 2 oz fresh
    ground lamb

1 large egg, beaten

2 tsp freshly squeezed
    lemon juice

$^1/_2$ tsp ground cumin

pinch of cayenne pepper,
    to taste

2 tbsp very finely chopped
    fresh mint

salt and pepper

300 ml/10 fl oz tomato &
    pepper salsa (see page
    56), to serve

method

1 Heat 1 tablespoon of olive oil in a frying pan over medium heat. Add the onion and cook for 5 minutes, stirring occasionally, until softened but not browned.

2 Remove the pan from the heat and let cool. Add the onion to the lamb with the egg, lemon juice, cumin, cayenne, mint, salt and pepper in a large bowl. Use your hands to squeeze all the ingredients together. Cook a small piece of the mixture and taste to see if the seasoning needs adjusting.

3 With wet hands, shape the mixture into about 60 x 2-cm/$^3/_4$-inch balls. Place on a tray and chill for at least 20 minutes.

4 When ready to cook, heat a small amount of olive oil in 1 or 2 large frying pans (the exact amount of oil will depend on how much fat is in the lamb). Arrange the meatballs in a single layer without overcrowding the pans and cook over medium heat for 5 minutes or until brown on the outside but still pink inside. Work in batches if necessary, keeping the cooked meatballs warm while you cook the remainder.

5 Gently reheat the tomato & pepper salsa and serve with the meatballs for dipping. These are best served warm with reheated sauce, but they are also enjoyable at room temperature.

mixed tapas platter with beef

ingredients

SERVES 8-10

200 g/7 oz small waxy
   potatoes, unpeeled

5 tbsp olive oil

2 sirloin steaks, about
   225 g/8 oz each

salt and pepper

1 fresh red chilli, deseeded
   and finely chopped
   (optional)

350 g/12 oz Queso del
   Montsec or other goat
   cheese, sliced

175 g/6 oz mixed salad leaves

2 tbsp black olives

2 tbsp green olives

55 g/2 oz canned anchovies
   in oil, drained and halved
   lengthways

1 tbsp capers, drained
   and rinsed

method

1 Cook the potatoes in a saucepan of lightly salted boiling water for 15–20 minutes or until just tender. Drain and cool slightly.

2 Heat a heavy-based frying pan or griddle pan over high heat and brush with 1 tablespoon of the olive oil. Season the steaks to taste with pepper and add to the pan. Cook for 1–1$^{1/2}$ minutes on each side, or until browned. Reduce the heat to medium and cook for 1$^{1/2}$ minutes on each side. Remove and rest for 10–15 minutes.

3 Heat 2 tablespoons of the remaining oil in a frying pan. Add the chilli, if using, and the potatoes and cook, turning frequently, for 10 minutes or until crisp and golden.

4 Thinly slice the steaks and arrange the slices alternately with the cheese slices along the sides of a serving platter. Mix the salad leaves, olives, anchovies and capers together, then arrange along the centre of the platter. Drizzle with the remaining oil, then top with the potatoes. Serve warm or at room temperature.

beef skewers with orange & garlic

ingredients

SERVES 6–8

3 tbsp white wine

2 tbsp olive oil

3 garlic cloves, finely chopped

juice of 1 orange

450 g/1 lb rump steak, cubed

salt and pepper

450 g/1 lb baby onions, halved

2 orange peppers, deseeded
  and cut into squares

225 g/8 oz cherry tomatoes,
  halved

method

1 Mix the wine, olive oil, garlic and orange juice together in a shallow, non-metallic dish. Add the cubes of steak, season to taste with salt and pepper and toss to coat. Cover with clingfilm and marinate in the refrigerator for 2–8 hours.

2 Preheat the grill to high. Drain the steak, reserving the marinade. Thread the steak, onions, peppers and tomatoes alternately onto several small skewers (see page 138 for tips on preparing skewers).

3 Cook the skewers under the hot grill, turning and brushing frequently with the marinade, for 10 minutes or until cooked through. Transfer to warmed serving plates and serve at once.

lamb skewers with lemon

ingredients

SERVES 8

2 garlic cloves,
   finely chopped

1 Spanish onion,
   finely chopped

2 tsp finely grated lemon rind

2 tbsp lemon juice

1 tsp fresh thyme leaves

1 tsp ground coriander

1 tsp ground cumin

2 tbsp red wine vinegar

125 ml/4 fl oz olive oil

1 kg/2 lb 4 oz lamb fillet, cut
   into 2-cm/³/₄-inch pieces

orange or lemon slices,
   to garnish

method

1 Mix the garlic, onion, lemon rind, lemon juice, thyme, coriander, cumin, vinegar and olive oil together in a large, shallow, non-metallic dish, whisking well until combined.

2 Thread the pieces of lamb onto 16 wooden skewers (see page 138 for tips on preparing skewers) and add to the dish, turning well to coat. Cover with clingfilm and marinate in the refrigerator for 2–8 hours, turning occasionally.

3 Preheat the grill to medium. Drain the skewers, reserving the marinade. Cook under the hot grill, turning frequently and brushing with the marinade, for 10 minutes or until tender and cooked to your liking. Serve immediately, garnished with orange slices.

miniature pork brochettes

ingredients

MAKES 12

450 g/1 lb lean boneless pork

3 tbsp Spanish olive oil, plus
	extra for oiling (optional)

grated rind and juice of
	1 large lemon

2 garlic cloves, crushed

2 tbsp chopped fresh
	flat-leaf parsley, plus extra
	to garnish

1 tbsp ras-el-hanout
	spice blend

salt and pepper

method

1 The brochettes are marinated overnight, so remember to do this in advance so that they are ready when you need them. Cut the pork into pieces about 2 cm/3/4 inch square and put in a large, shallow, non-metallic dish that will hold the pieces in a single layer.

2 To prepare the marinade, put the remaining ingredients in a bowl and mix well together. Pour the marinade over the pork and toss the meat in it until well coated. Cover the dish and marinate in the refrigerator for 8 hours or overnight, stirring the pork 2–3 times.

3 Preheat the grill, griddle pan, or barbecue. Thread 3 marinated pork pieces, leaving a little space between each piece, onto each prepared skewer. Cook the brochettes for 10–15 minutes or until tender and lightly charred, turning several times and basting with the remaining marinade during cooking. Serve the pork brochettes piping hot, garnished with parsley.

4 You can use wooden or metal skewers to cook the brochettes and for this recipe you will need about 12 x 15-cm/6-inch skewers. If you are using wooden ones, soak them in cold water for about 30 minutes prior to using. This helps to stop them burning and the food sticking to them during cooking. Metal skewers simply need to be greased and flat ones should be used in preference to round ones to prevent the food on them falling off.

chicken livers in sherry sauce

ingredients

SERVES 6

450 g/1 lb chicken livers

2 tbsp Spanish olive oil

1 small onion, finely chopped

2 garlic cloves, finely chopped

100 ml/3$\frac{1}{2}$ fl oz dry Spanish
    sherry

salt and pepper

2 tbsp chopped fresh
    flat-leaf parsley

crusty bread or toast, to serve

method

1 If necessary, trim the chicken livers, cutting away any ducts and gristle, then cut them into small, bite-size pieces.

2 Heat the olive oil in a large, heavy-based frying pan. Add the onion and cook for about 5 minutes or until softened but not browned. Add the garlic to the pan and cook for a further 30 seconds.

3 Add the chicken livers to the pan and cook for 2–3 minutes, stirring all the time, until they are firm and have changed colour on the outside but are still pink and soft in the centre. Using a slotted spoon, lift the chicken livers from the pan, transfer them to a large, warmed serving dish and keep warm.

4 Add the sherry to the frying pan, increase the heat and let it bubble for 3–4 minutes to evaporate the alcohol and reduce slightly. At the same time, deglaze the frying pan by scraping and stirring all the bits on the bottom of the pan into the sauce with a wooden spoon. Season to taste with salt and pepper.

5 Pour the sherry sauce over the chicken livers and sprinkle over the parsley. Serve piping hot, with chunks or slices of crusty bread or toast to mop up the sherry sauce.

chicken rolls with olives

ingredients

SERVES 6–8

115 g/4 oz black olives
    in oil, drained

140 g/5 oz butter, softened

4 tbsp chopped fresh parsley

4 skinless, boneless
    chicken breasts

2 tbsp oil from the olive jar

method

1 Preheat the oven to 200°C/400°F. Pit and chop the olives. Mix half the olives, the butter and the parsley together in a bowl.

2 Place the chicken breasts between 2 sheets of clingfilm and beat gently with a meat mallet or the side of rolling pin.

3 Spread the olive and herb butter over one side of each flattened chicken breast and roll up. Secure with a wooden cocktail stick or tie with clean string if necessary.

4 Place the chicken rolls in an ovenproof dish. Drizzle over the oil from the olive jar and bake in the preheated oven for 45–55 minutes or until tender and the juices run clear when the chicken is pierced with the point of a sharp knife.

5 Transfer the chicken rolls to a cutting board and discard the cocktail sticks or string. Using a sharp knife, cut into slices, then transfer to warmed serving plates and serve.

chicken in lemon & garlic

ingredients

SERVES 6–8

4 large skinless, boneless
   chicken breasts

5 tbsp Spanish olive oil

1 onion, finely chopped

6 garlic cloves,
   finely chopped

grated rind of 1 lemon, finely
   pared rind of 1 lemon and
   juice of both lemons

4 tbsp chopped fresh
   flat-leaf parsley, plus extra
   to garnish

salt and pepper

lemon wedges and crusty
   bread, to serve

method

1 Using a sharp knife, slice the chicken breasts widthways into very thin slices. Heat the olive oil in a large, heavy-based frying pan, add the onion and cook for 5 minutes or until softened but not browned. Add the garlic and cook for an additional 30 seconds.

2 Add the sliced chicken to the frying pan and cook gently for 5–10 minutes, stirring from time to time, until all the ingredients are lightly browned and the chicken is tender.

3 Add the grated lemon rind and the lemon juice and let it bubble. At the same time, deglaze the frying pan by scraping and stirring all the bits on the bottom of the pan into the juices with a wooden spoon. Remove the pan from the heat, stir in the parsley and season to taste with salt and pepper.

4 Transfer, piping hot, to a warmed serving dish. Sprinkle with the pared lemon rind, garnish with the parsley and serve with lemon wedges for squeezing over the chicken, accompanied by chunks or slices of crusty bread for mopping up the juices.

for seafood fans

Spain is bordered by the Atlantic and Mediterranean seas, so fresh fish and shellfish are eaten in vast quantities in this country. You only have to pay a visit to a Spanish fish market to see the incredible array of different varieties and, needless to say, they are the pride of Spanish tapas. This chapter has a selection of the best recipes and it is worth spending a little extra on top-quality fresh ingredients, even if it is only on special occasions. When you bite into a chunk of monkfish or a sizzling giant garlic prawn, you will understand why.

Prawns are enjoyed throughout the whole of Spain and there will be a prawn dish or two on almost all tapas menus. Its popularity is very much in evidence in the older-style Spanish tapas bars, and one good reason for this is that, apart from the occasional fork, cutlery is not involved in eating tapas, so prawns are shelled with enthusiasm and the shell discarded on the floor along with lemon seeds, cocktail sticks, and paper napkins. A covering of sawdust on the floor is often provided for this very reason!

Many of these dishes work very well as smart, elegant first courses – adjust the quantities if necessary to suit the number of servings you require.

monkfish, rosemary & bacon skewers

ingredients

MAKES 12

250 g/9 oz monkfish fillet

12 stalks of fresh rosemary

3 tbsp Spanish olive oil

juice of $\frac{1}{2}$ small lemon

1 garlic clove, crushed

salt and pepper

6 thick slices Canadian bacon

lemon wedges, to garnish

aïoli, to serve (see page 70)

method

1 Slice the monkfish fillets in half lengthways, then cut each fillet into 12 bite-size chunks to make a total of 24 pieces. Put the monkfish pieces in a large bowl.

2 To prepare the rosemary skewers, strip the leaves off the stalks and set them aside, leaving a few leaves at one end.

3 For the marinade, finely chop the reserved leaves and whisk together in a bowl with the olive oil, lemon juice, garlic, salt and pepper. Add the monkfish pieces and toss until coated in the marinade. Cover and marinate in the refrigerator for 1–2 hours.

4 Cut each bacon slice in half lengthways, then in half widthways, and roll up each piece. Thread 2 pieces of monkfish alternately with 2 bacon rolls onto each rosemary skewer.

5 Preheat the grill, griddle pan, or barbecue. If you are cooking the skewers under a grill, arrange them on the grill pan so that the leaves of the rosemary skewers protrude from the grill and do not catch fire. Grill the skewers for 10 minutes or until cooked, turning from time to time and basting with any remaining marinade. Serve hot, garnished with lemon wedges, with a bowl of aïoli.

traditional catalan salt cod salad

ingredients

SERVES 4–6

400 g/14 oz dried salt cod
   in 1 piece

6 spring onions, thinly sliced
   on the diagonal

6 tbsp extra virgin olive oil

1 tbsp sherry vinegar

1 tbsp lemon juice

pepper

2 large red peppers, grilled,
   peeled, deseeded and
   very finely diced

12 large black olives, pitted
   and sliced

2 large, juicy tomatoes,
   thinly sliced

2 tbsp very finely chopped
   fresh parsley, to garnish

method

1 Place the dried salt cod in a large bowl, then cover with cold water and soak for 48 hours, changing the water 3 times a day.

2 Pat the salt cod very dry with kitchen paper and remove the skin and bones, then use your fingers to tear into fine shreds. Place in a large, non-metallic bowl with the spring onions, olive oil, vinegar and lemon juice and toss together. Season with pepper, then cover and marinate in the refrigerator for 3 hours.

3 Stir in the peppers and olives. Taste and adjust the seasoning, if necessary, remembering that the cod and olives might be salty. Arrange the tomato slices on a large serving platter or individual serving plates and spoon the salad on top. Sprinkle with chopped parsley and serve.

cod & caper croquettes

ingredients

MAKES 12

350 g/12 oz white fish fillets,
    such as cod, haddock,
    or monkfish, skinned
    and boned
300 ml/10 fl oz milk
salt and pepper
4 tbsp olive oil or
    55 g/2 oz butter
55 g/2 oz plain flour
4 tbsp capers,
    roughly chopped
1 tsp paprika
1 garlic clove, crushed
1 tsp lemon juice
3 tbsp chopped fresh
    flat-leaf parsley, plus extra
    sprigs to garnish
1 egg, beaten
55 g/2 oz fresh white
    breadcrumbs
1 tbsp sesame seeds
corn oil, for deep-frying
lemon wedges, to garnish
mayonnaise, to serve

method

1 Put the fish fillets and milk in a large frying pan and season to taste. Bring to the boil, then lower the heat, cover, and cook for 8–10 minutes or until the fish flakes easily. Remove the fish, reserving the milk. Flake the fish.

2 Heat the olive oil or butter in a saucepan. Stir in the flour to form a paste and cook gently, stirring, for 1 minute. Gradually stir in the reserved milk until smooth. Slowly bring to the boil, stirring, until the mixture thickens.

3 Remove from the heat, add the flaked fish and beat until smooth. Add the capers, paprika, garlic, lemon juice and parsley and mix well. Season to taste. Transfer to a dish and cool. Cover and chill for 2–3 hours.

4 Pour the beaten egg onto a plate. Combine the breadcrumbs and sesame seeds on a separate plate. Divide the fish mixture into 12 portions and form each portion into a 7.5-cm/3-inch sausage shape. Dip each croquette in the beaten egg, then coat it in the breadcrumb mixture. Chill for 1 hour.

5 Heat the oil in a deep-fryer to 180–190°C/350–375°F. Cook the croquettes, in batches, for 3 minutes, or until golden brown and crispy. Drain well on kitchen paper.

6 Serve piping hot, garnished with lemon wedges and parsley sprigs and accompanied by a bowl of mayonnaise for dipping.

salt cod & avocado

ingredients

SERVES 6

350 g/12 oz dried salt cod

2 tbsp olive oil

1 onion, finely chopped

1 garlic clove, finely chopped

3 avocados

1 tbsp lemon juice

pinch of chilli powder

1 tbsp dry sherry

4 tbsp double cream

salt and pepper

method

1 Soak the dried salt cod in cold water for 48 hours, changing the water 3 times a day. Drain well and pat dry on kitchen paper, then chop into large chunks.

2 Preheat the oven to 180°C/350°F. Heat the olive oil in a large, heavy-based frying pan. Add the onion and garlic and cook over low heat, stirring occasionally, for 5 minutes, or until softened. Add the fish and cook over medium heat, stirring frequently, for 6–8 minutes, or until the fish flakes easily. Remove from the heat and cool slightly.

3 Meanwhile, halve the avocados lengthways and remove and discard the stones. Using a teaspoon, carefully scoop out the flesh without piercing the skins. Reserve the skins and mash the flesh with the lemon juice in a bowl.

4 Remove and discard any skin and bones from the fish, then add the fish mixture to the avocado, together with the chilli powder, sherry and cream. Beat well with a fork and season to taste with salt and pepper.

5 Spoon the mixture into the avocado skins and place them on a baking sheet. Bake in the preheated oven for 10–15 minutes, then transfer to warmed serving plates and serve.

catalan fish

ingredients

SERVES 4

4 globe artichokes, stems
    cut off, tough outer
    leaves removed and
    discarded, and points of
    the leaves trimmed with
    kitchen scissors

2 soles, filleted

$1/2$ lemon

225 ml/8 fl oz dry white wine

55 g/2 oz butter

2 tbsp plain flour

225 ml/8 fl oz milk

salt and pepper

freshly grated nutmeg

bay leaf

115 g/4 oz sliced mushrooms

method

1 Put the artichokes in a saucepan. Add water to cover and a pinch of salt. Bring to the boil, then simmer for 30 minutes or until tender.

2 Season the fish fillets to taste and squeeze over the lemon. Cut each fillet into quarters lengthways, roll up and secure with a cocktail stick. Place in a shallow saucepan, then pour in the wine and poach gently, spooning over the wine occasionally, for 15 minutes.

3 Melt half the butter in a separate saucepan, then add the flour and cook, stirring, for 2 minutes. Gradually stir in the milk. Bring to the boil, stirring constantly, until thickened and smooth. Reduce the heat to very low, season to taste with salt, pepper and nutmeg and add the bay leaf.

4 Melt the remaining butter in a frying pan. Add the mushrooms and cook over medium heat, stirring occasionally, for 3 minutes. Remove the frying pan from the heat.

5 Remove the artichokes from the pan with a slotted spoon and drain on kitchen paper. Remove and discard the hairy chokes and prickly leaves. Divide the mushrooms between the artichoke cavities and spoon in the sauce, discarding the bay leaf. Drain the fish fillets with a slotted spoon and remove and discard the cocktail sticks. Place two fillets in each of the artichoke cavities and serve.

sardines with lemon & chilli

ingredients

SERVES 4

450 g/1 lb fresh sardines,
    scaled, cleaned and
    heads removed
4 tbsp lemon juice
1 garlic clove, finely chopped
1 tbsp finely chopped fresh dill
1 tsp finely chopped
    fresh red chilli
salt and pepper
4 tbsp olive oil

method

1 Place the sardines, skin-side up, on a cutting board and press along the length of the spines with your thumbs. Turn them over and remove and discard the bones.

2 Place the fillets, skin-side down, in a shallow, non-metallic dish and sprinkle with the lemon juice. Cover with clingfilm and stand in a cool place for 30 minutes.

3 Drain off any excess lemon juice. Sprinkle the garlic, dill and chilli over the fish and season to taste with salt and pepper. Drizzle over the olive oil, then cover with clingfilm and chill for 12 hours before serving.

sardines marinated in sherry vinegar

ingredients

SERVES 6

12 small fresh sardines,
    cleaned and filleted, and
    heads and tails removed
    if wished
175 ml/6 fl oz Spanish
    olive oil
4 tbsp sherry vinegar
2 carrots, cut into julienne strips
1 onion, thinly sliced
1 garlic clove, crushed
1 bay leaf
salt and pepper
4 tbsp chopped fresh
    flat-leaf parsley
few sprigs of fresh dill,
    to garnish
lemon wedges, to serve

method

1 Heat 4 tablespoons of the olive oil in a large, heavy-based frying pan. Add the sardines and cook for 10 minutes or until browned on both sides. Using a spatula, very carefully remove the sardines from the pan and transfer to a large, shallow, non-metallic dish that will hold the sardines in a single layer.

2 Gently heat the remaining olive oil and the sherry vinegar in a large saucepan, add the carrot strips, onion, garlic and bay leaf and simmer gently for 5 minutes or until softened. Season the vegetables to taste with salt and pepper. Allow the mixture to cool slightly, then pour the marinade over the sardines.

3 Cover the dish and allow the sardines to cool before transferring to the refrigerator. Marinate for about 8 hours or overnight, spooning the marinade over the sardines occasionally. Return the sardines to room temperature before serving. Sprinkle with parsley, garnish with dill sprigs and serve with lemon wedges.

sardines with romesco sauce

ingredients

SERVES 6

24 fresh sardines, scaled,
   cleaned, filleted, and
   heads removed
115 g/4 oz plain flour
4 eggs, lightly beaten
250 g/9 oz fresh white
   breadcrumbs
6 tbsp chopped fresh parsley
4 tbsp chopped
   fresh marjoram
vegetable oil, for deep-frying

romesco sauce

1 red pepper, halved
   and deseeded
2 tomatoes, halved
4 garlic cloves
125 ml/4 fl oz olive oil
1 slice white bread, diced
4 tbsp blanched almonds
1 fresh red chilli, deseeded
   and chopped
2 shallots, chopped
1 tsp paprika
2 tbsp red wine vinegar
2 tsp sugar
1 tbsp water

method

1 To make the sauce, place the pepper, tomatoes and garlic in an ovenproof dish and drizzle over 1 tablespoon of the olive oil, turning to coat. Bake in a preheated oven, 220°C/425°F, for 20–25 minutes. Remove and set aside to cool, then peel off their skins and place the flesh in a food processor.

2 Heat 1 tablespoon of the remaining oil in a frying pan. Add the bread and almonds and cook over low heat for a few minutes until browned. Remove and drain on kitchen paper. Add the chilli, shallots and paprika to the pan and cook until the shallots are softened.

3 Transfer the almond and shallot mixtures to the food processor and add the vinegar, sugar and water. Process to a paste. With the motor still running, gradually add the remaining oil through the feeder tube. Transfer to a bowl, cover and reserve.

4 Place the flour and eggs in separate bowls. Mix the breadcrumbs and herbs together in a third bowl. Toss the sardines in the flour, then the eggs, then the breadcrumbs.

5 Heat the vegetable oil in a large pan until a cube of bread browns in 30 seconds. Deep-fry the fish for 4–5 minutes or until golden and tender. Drain and serve with the sauce.

pickled mackerel

ingredients

SERVES 6

8 fresh mackerel fillets

300 ml/10 fl oz extra-virgin
   olive oil

2 large red onions, thinly sliced

2 carrots, sliced

2 bay leaves

2 garlic cloves, thinly sliced

2 dried red chillies

1 fennel bulb, halved and
   thinly sliced

300 ml/10 fl oz sherry vinegar

1$\frac{1}{2}$ tbsp coriander seeds

salt and pepper

toasted French bread slices,
   to serve

method

1 Preheat the grill to medium. Place the mackerel fillets, skin-side up, on a grill rack and brush with oil. Cook under the hot grill, about 10 cm/4 inches from the heat source, for 4–6 minutes or until the skins become brown and crispy and the flesh flakes easily. Reserve until required.

2 Heat the remaining oil in a large frying pan. Add the onions and cook for 5 minutes or until softened but not browned. Add the remaining ingredients and simmer for 10 minutes or until the carrots are tender.

3 Flake the mackerel flesh into large pieces, removing the skin and tiny bones. Place the mackerel pieces in a preserving jar and pour over the onion, carrot and fennel mixture. (The jar should accommodate everything packed in quite tightly with the minimum air gap at the top once the vegetable mixture has been poured in.) Cool completely, then cover tightly and chill for at least 24 hours and up to 5 days. Serve the pieces of mackerel on toasted slices of French bread with a little of the oil drizzled over.

4 Alternatively, serve the mackerel and its pickled vegetables as a first-course salad.

fresh salmon in mojo sauce

ingredients

SERVES 8

4 fresh salmon fillets,
    weighing about 750 g/
    1 lb 10 oz in total
salt and pepper
3 tbsp Spanish olive oil
1 fresh flat-leaf parsley sprig,
    to garnish

mojo sauce

2 garlic cloves, peeled
2 tsp paprika
1 tsp ground cumin
5 tbsp Spanish extra-virgin
    olive oil
2 tbsp white wine vinegar
salt

method

1 To prepare the mojo sauce, put the garlic, paprika and cumin in the bowl of a food processor fitted with the metal blade and, using a pulsing action, blend for 1 minute to mix well together. With the motor running, add 1 tablespoon of the olive oil, drop by drop, through the feeder tube. When it has been added, scrape down the sides of the bowl with a spatula, then very slowly continue to pour in the oil in a thin steady stream, until all the oil has been added and the sauce has slightly thickened. Add the vinegar and blend for an additional 1 minute. Season the sauce with salt to taste.

2 To prepare the salmon, remove the skin, cut each fillet in half widthways, then cut lengthways into 2-cm/3/4-inch thick slices, discarding any bones. Season the pieces of fish to taste with salt and pepper.

3 Heat the olive oil in a large, heavy-based frying pan. When hot, add the pieces of fish and cook for about 10 minutes, depending on its thickness, turning occasionally until cooked and browned on both sides.

4 Transfer the salmon to a warmed serving dish, drizzle over some of the mojo sauce and serve hot, garnished with parsley and accompanied by the remaining sauce in a small serving bowl.

tuna, egg & potato salad

ingredients

SERVES 4

350 g/12 oz new potatoes, unpeeled

1 hard-boiled egg, cooled and shelled

3 tbsp olive oil

1½ tbsp white wine vinegar

salt and pepper

115 g/4 oz canned tuna in oil, drained and flaked

2 shallots, finely chopped

1 tomato, peeled and diced

2 tbsp chopped fresh parsley

method

1 Cook the potatoes in a saucepan of lightly salted boiling water for 10 minutes, then remove from the heat, cover and stand for 15–20 minutes or until tender.

2 Meanwhile, slice the egg, then cut each slice in half. Whisk the olive oil and vinegar together in a bowl and season to taste with salt and pepper. Spoon a little of the vinaigrette into a serving dish to coat the base.

3 Drain the potatoes, then peel and thinly slice. Place half the slices over the base of the dish and season to taste with salt, then top with half the tuna, half the egg slices and half the shallots. Pour over half the remaining dressing. Make a second layer with the remaining potato slices, tuna, egg and shallots, then pour over the remaining dressing.

4 Finally, top the salad with the tomato and parsley. Cover with clingfilm and stand in a cool place for 1–2 hours before serving.

tuna with pimiento-stuffed olives

ingredients

SERVES 6

2 fresh tuna steaks,
    weighing about 250 g/
    9 oz in total and about
    2.5 cm/1 inch thick
5 tbsp Spanish olive oil
3 tbsp red wine vinegar
4 sprigs of fresh thyme,
    plus extra to garnish
1 bay leaf
salt and pepper
2 tbsp plain flour
1 onion, finely chopped
2 garlic cloves, finely chopped
85 g/3 oz pimiento-stuffed
    green olives, sliced
crusty bread, to serve

method

1 Remove the skin from the tuna steaks, then cut the steaks in half along the grain of the fish. Cut each half into 1-cm/^{1}/$_2$-inch thick slices against the grain.

2 Put 3 tablespoons of the olive oil and the vinegar in a large, shallow, non-metallic dish. Strip the leaves from the sprigs of thyme and add these to the dish with the bay leaf and salt and pepper to taste. Add the prepared strips of tuna, cover the dish and marinate in the refrigerator overnight.

3 Put the flour in a plastic bag. Remove the tuna strips from the marinade, reserving the marinade for later, add them to the bag of flour and toss well until lightly coated.

4 Heat the remaining olive oil in a large frying pan. Add the onion and garlic and gently cook for 5–10 minutes or until softened and golden brown. Add the tuna strips and cook for 2–5 minutes, turning several times, until the fish becomes opaque. Add the reserved marinade and olives to the pan and cook for a further 1–2 minutes, stirring, until the fish is tender and the sauce has thickened.

5 Serve the tuna and olives piping hot, garnished with thyme sprigs. Accompany with chunks or slices of crusty bread.

tuna rolls

ingredients

SERVES 4

3 red peppers

125 ml/4 fl oz olive oil

2 tbsp lemon juice

5 tbsp red wine vinegar

2 garlic cloves, finely chopped

1 tsp paprika

1 tsp dried chilli flakes

2 tsp sugar

2 tbsp salted capers

200 g/7 oz canned tuna in oil,
   drained and flaked

method

1 Preheat the grill to high. Place the peppers on a baking sheet and cook under the preheated grill, turning frequently, for 10 minutes or until the skin is blackened and blistered all over. Using tongs, transfer to a plastic bag, then tie the top and cool.

2 Meanwhile, whisk the olive oil, lemon juice, vinegar, garlic, paprika, chilli flakes and sugar together in a small bowl.

3 When the peppers are cool enough to handle, peel off the skins, then cut the flesh into thirds lengthways and deseed. Place the pepper pieces in a non-metallic dish and pour over the dressing, turning to coat. Stand in a cool place for 30 minutes.

4 Rub the salt off the capers and mix with the tuna. Drain the pepper pieces, reserving the dressing. Divide the tuna mixture between the pepper pieces and roll up. Secure with a wooden cocktail stick. Place the tuna rolls on a serving platter, then spoon over the dressing and serve at room temperature.

empanadillas

ingredients

SERVES 6–8

2 tbsp olive oil, plus extra
    for brushing
500 g/1 lb 2 oz fresh
    spinach leaves
2 garlic cloves, finely chopped
8 canned anchovy fillets in oil,
    drained and chopped
2 tbsp raisins, soaked in hot
    water for 10 minutes
40 g/1^{1}/$_{2}$ oz pine nuts
450 g/1 lb puff pastry,
    thawed if frozen
plain flour, for dusting
1 egg, lightly beaten
salt and pepper

method

1 Preheat the oven to 180°C/350°F. Lightly brush 1–2 baking sheets with olive oil.

2 Trim and discard any tough stems from the spinach and finely chop the leaves.

3 Heat the olive oil in a large saucepan. Add the chopped spinach, then cover and cook over low heat, gently shaking the pan occasionally, for 3 minutes. Stir in the garlic and anchovies and cook, uncovered, for a further 1 minute. Remove from the heat.

4 Drain the raisins and chop, then stir them into the spinach mixture with the pine nuts and salt and pepper to taste. Allow to cool.

5 Roll out the pastry on a lightly floured work surface to a circle about 3 mm/^{1}/$_{8}$ inch thick. Stamp out circles using a 7.5-cm/3-inch biscuit cutter. Re-roll the trimmings and stamp out more circles.

6 Place 1–2 heaped teaspoonfuls of the spinach filling onto each pastry round. Brush the edges with water and fold over to make half moons. Press together well to seal. Place the empanadillas on the baking trays and brush with beaten egg to glaze, then bake in the preheated oven for 15 minutes or until golden brown. Serve warm.

squid & beans

ingredients

SERVES 6

500 g/1 lb 2 oz prepared
    squid

3 garlic cloves, chopped

300 ml/10 fl oz dry red wine

salt and pepper

500 g/1 lb 2 oz new potatoes,
    unpeeled

225 g/8 oz green beans,
    cut into short lengths

4 tbsp olive oil

1 tbsp red wine vinegar

method

1 Preheat the oven to 180°C/350°F. Using a sharp knife, cut the squid into rings about 1 cm/$1/2$ inch thick and place them in an ovenproof dish. Sprinkle with half the garlic, then pour over the wine and season to taste with salt and pepper. Cover the dish with foil and bake in the preheated oven for 45–50 minutes or until the squid feels tender when pierced with the point of a sharp knife.

2 Meanwhile, cook the potatoes in a saucepan of lightly salted boiling water for 15–20 minutes or until tender. Drain and set aside to cool slightly, then thickly slice and place in a large bowl.

3 Cook the beans in a separate saucepan of lightly salted boiling water for 3–5 minutes or until tender. Drain and add to the potatoes. Drain the squid and add to the bowl.

4 Whisk the olive oil, vinegar and remaining garlic together in a bowl and season to taste with salt and pepper. Pour the dressing over the salad and toss lightly. Divide the salad between individual serving plates and serve warm.

calamares

ingredients

SERVES 6

450 g/1 lb prepared squid

plain flour, for coating

corn oil, for deep-frying

salt

lemon wedges, to garnish

aïoli, to serve (see page 70)

method

1 Slice the squid into 1-cm/$\frac{1}{2}$-inch rings and halve the tentacles, if large. Rinse and dry well on kitchen paper so that they do not spit during cooking. Dust the squid rings with flour so that they are lightly coated. Do not season the flour, as this will toughen the squid.

2 Heat the oil in a deep-fryer to 180–190°C/350–375°F or until a cube of bread browns in 30 seconds. Carefully add the squid rings, in batches so that the temperature of the oil does not drop, and deep-fry for 2–3 minutes or until golden brown and crisp all over, turning several times. Do not overcook as the squid will become tough and rubbery rather than moist and tender.

3 Using a slotted spoon, remove the deep-fried squid from the deep-fryer and drain well on kitchen paper. Transfer to a warm oven while you deep-fry the remaining squid rings.

4 Sprinkle the deep-fried squid with salt and serve piping hot, garnished with lemon wedges for squeezing over them. Accompany with a bowl of aïoli in which to dip the pieces.

giant garlic prawns

ingredients

SERVES 4

125 ml/4 fl oz olive oil

4 garlic cloves, finely chopped

2 hot fresh red chillies,
    deseeded and finely
    chopped

450 g/1 lb cooked
    king prawns

2 tbsp chopped fresh
    flat-leaf parsley

salt and pepper

lemon wedges, to garnish

crusty bread, to serve

method

1 Heat the olive oil in a preheated wok or large, heavy-based frying pan over low heat. Add the garlic and chillies and cook, stirring occasionally, for 1–2 minutes or until softened but not coloured.

2 Add the prawns and stir-fry for 2–3 minutes or until heated through and coated in the oil and garlic mixture.

3 Turn off the heat and add the chopped parsley, stirring well to mix. Season to taste with salt and pepper.

4 Divide the prawns and garlic-flavoured oil between warmed serving dishes and garnish with lemon wedges. Serve with crusty bread.

lime-drizzled prawns

ingredients

SERVES 6

4 limes

12 raw king prawns,
   in their shells

3 tbsp Spanish olive oil

2 garlic cloves, finely chopped

splash of fino sherry

salt and pepper

4 tbsp chopped fresh
   flat-leaf parsley

method

1 Grate the rind and squeeze the juice from 2 of the limes. Cut the remaining 2 limes into wedges and set aside for later.

2 To prepare the prawns, remove the head and legs, leaving the shells and tails intact. Using a sharp knife, make a shallow slit along the back of each prawn, then pull out the dark vein and discard. Rinse the prawns under cold water and dry on kitchen paper.

3 Heat the olive oil in a large, heavy-based frying pan, then add the garlic and cook for 30 seconds. Add the prawns and cook for 5 minutes, stirring from time to time, or until they turn pink and start to curl. Mix in the lime rind and juice and a splash of sherry to moisten, then stir well together.

4 Transfer the cooked prawns to a serving dish, season to taste with salt and pepper, and sprinkle with the parsley. Serve piping hot, accompanied by the reserved lime wedges for squeezing over the prawns.

prawns with saffron dressing

ingredients

SERVES 6–8

large pinch of saffron threads

2 tbsp warm water

150 ml/5 fl oz mayonnaise

2 tbsp grated onion

4 tbsp lemon juice

1 tsp Dijon mustard

salt and pepper

1 kg/2 lb 4 oz cooked
    Mediterranean prawns

1 cos lettuce, separated
    into leaves

4 tomatoes, cut into wedges

8 black olives

method

1 Stir the saffron with the water in a small bowl. Gently whisk the mayonnaise, onion, lemon juice and mustard together in a separate, non-metallic bowl until thoroughly combined. Season to taste with salt and pepper and stir in the saffron soaking liquid. Cover with clingfilm and chill.

2 Pull the heads off the prawns and peel. Cut along the length of the back of each prawn and remove and discard the dark vein. Rinse and pat dry with kitchen paper.

3 Arrange the lettuce leaves on a large serving platter or on individual serving plates. Top with the prawns and scatter with the tomato wedges and olives. Serve with the saffron dressing.

garlic prawns with lemon & parsley

ingredients

SERVES 6

60 raw jumbo prawns,
    thawed if using frozen
150 ml/5 fl oz olive oil
6 garlic cloves, thinly sliced
3 dried hot red chillies
    (optional)
6 tbsp freshly squeezed
    lemon juice
6 tbsp very finely chopped
    fresh parsley
french bread, to serve

method

1 Peel and devein the prawns and remove the heads, leaving the tails on. Rinse and pat the prawns dry.

2 Heat the olive oil in a large, deep sauté pan or frying pan. Add the garlic and chillies, if using, and stir constantly until they begin to sizzle. Add the prawns and cook until they turn pink and begin to curl.

3 Use a slotted spoon to transfer the prawns to warm earthenware bowls. Sprinkle each bowl with lemon juice and parsley. Serve with plenty of bread to mop up the juices.

cidered scallops

ingredients

SERVES 4–5

1 litre/1 3/4 pints dry cider

4 tbsp lemon juice

salt and pepper

20 scallops, shelled

85 g/3 oz butter

2 tbsp plain flour

225 ml/8 fl oz sour cream

115 g/4 oz white mushrooms

method

1 Preheat the oven to 110°C/225°F. Pour the cider and lemon juice into a large, shallow pan and season to taste with salt and pepper. Add the scallops and poach for 10 minutes or until tender. Using a slotted spoon, transfer the scallops to an ovenproof dish. Dot with 2 tablespoons of the butter, then cover with foil and keep warm in the oven.

2 Bring the scallop cooking liquid to the boil and continue to boil until reduced by about half. Mix together 2 tablespoons of the remaining butter and the flour, mashing well with a fork to make a paste. Beat the paste, a little at a time, into the liquid until thickened and smooth. Stir in the sour cream and simmer gently for 5–10 minutes.

3 Taste the sauce and adjust the seasoning if necessary. Remove the scallops from the oven and return them to the pan, then heat through for 2–3 minutes.

4 Meanwhile, melt the remaining butter in a small frying pan. Add the mushrooms and cook over low heat, stirring frequently, for 2–3 minutes. Add them to the pan of scallops, then transfer to individual serving dishes and serve.

baked scallops

ingredients

SERVES 4

700 g/1 lb 9 oz scallops,
    shelled and chopped

2 onions, finely chopped

2 garlic cloves, finely chopped

3 tbsp chopped fresh parsley

pinch of freshly grated nutmeg

pinch of ground cloves

salt and pepper

2 tbsp fresh white
    breadcrumbs

2 tbsp olive oil

method

1 Preheat the oven to 200°C/400°F. Mix the scallops, onions, garlic, 2 tablespoons of the parsley, the nutmeg and cloves together in a bowl and season to taste with salt and pepper.

2 Divide the mixture between 4 scrubbed scallop shells or heatproof dishes. Sprinkle the breadcrumbs and remaining parsley on top and drizzle with the olive oil.

3 Bake the scallops in the preheated oven for 15–20 minutes or until lightly golden and piping hot. Serve immediately.

scallops in saffron sauce

ingredients

SERVES 8

150 ml/5 fl oz dry white wine

150 ml/5 fl oz fish stock

large pinch of saffron threads

900 g/2 lb scallops,
    preferably large ones,
    shelled

salt and pepper

3 tbsp Spanish olive oil

1 small onion, finely chopped

2 garlic cloves, finely chopped

150 ml/5 fl oz double cream

squeeze of lemon juice

chopped fresh flat-leaf
    parsley, to garnish

crusty bread, to serve

method

1 Put the wine, fish stock and saffron in a saucepan and bring to the boil. Lower the heat, cover, and simmer gently for 15 minutes.

2 Meanwhile, remove and discard from each scallop the tough, white muscle that is found opposite the coral, and separate the coral from the scallop. Slice the scallops and corals vertically into thick slices. Dry well on kitchen paper, then season to taste.

3 Heat the olive oil in a large, heavy-based frying pan. Add the onion and garlic and cook until softened and lightly browned. Add the sliced scallops to the pan and cook gently for 5 minutes, stirring occasionally, or until they turn just opaque. Overcooking the scallops will make them tough and rubbery.

4 Using a slotted spoon, remove the scallops from the frying pan and transfer to a warmed plate. Add the saffron liquid to the pan, bring to the boil and boil rapidly until reduced to about half. Lower the heat and gradually stir in the cream, just a little at a time. Simmer gently until the sauce thickens.

5 Return the scallops to the pan and simmer for 1–2 minutes just to heat through. Add a squeeze of lemon juice and season to taste with salt and pepper. Serve the scallops hot, garnished with the parsley, with slices or chunks of crusty bread.

seared scallops

ingredients

SERVES 4–6

4 tbsp olive oil

3 tbsp orange juice

2 tsp hazelnut oil

salt and pepper

24 scallops, shelled

salad leaves (optional)

175 g/6 oz Cabrales or other
  blue cheese, crumbled

2 tbsp chopped fresh dill

1 Whisk 3 tablespoons of the olive oil, the orange juice and the hazelnut oil together in a jug and season to taste with salt and pepper.

2 Heat the remaining olive oil in a large, heavy-based frying pan. Add the scallops and cook over high heat for 1 minute on each side, or until golden.

3 Transfer the scallops to a bed of salad leaves or individual plates. Scatter over the cheese and dill, then drizzle with the dressing and serve warm.

scallops with serrano ham

ingredients

SERVES 4

2 tbsp lemon juice

3 tbsp olive oil

2 garlic cloves, finely chopped

1 tbsp chopped fresh parsley

12 scallops, preferably with
corals, shelled

16 wafer-thin slices
serrano ham

pepper

method

1 Mix the lemon juice, olive oil, garlic and parsley together in a non-metallic dish. Separate the corals, if using, from the scallops and add both to the dish, turning to coat. Cover with clingfilm and marinate at room temperature for 20 minutes.

2 Preheat the grill to medium. Drain the scallops, reserving the marinade. Scrunch up a slice of ham and thread it onto a metal skewer, followed by a scallop and a coral, if using, finishing with a scrunched-up slice of ham. Repeat to fill 4 skewers with the ham, scallops and corals.

3 Cook under the hot grill, basting with the marinade and turning frequently, for 5 minutes or until the scallops are tender and the ham is crisp.

4 Transfer to warmed serving plates and sprinkle with pepper. Spoon over the cooking juices from the grill pan and serve.

crab with almonds

ingredients

SERVES 4

450 g/1 lb fresh, canned or
     frozen crabmeat, thawed
115 g/4 oz butter
85 g/3 oz flaked almonds
salt and pepper
125 ml/4 fl oz double cream
1 tbsp chopped fresh parsley

method

1 Remove any pieces of cartilage or shell from the crabmeat. Melt half the butter in a heavy-based frying pan. Add the crabmeat and cook over medium heat, stirring occasionally, for 10 minutes or until browned. Remove the pan from the heat and reserve.

2 Melt the remaining butter in a separate frying pan. Add the almonds and cook over low heat, stirring occasionally, for 5 minutes or until golden brown.

3 Stir the almonds into the crabmeat and season to taste with salt and pepper. Stir in the cream and parsley and bring to the boil. Reduce the heat and simmer for 3 minutes. Transfer to a warmed serving dish and serve immediately.

clams with broad beans

ingredients

SERVES 4–6

4 canned anchovy fillets
    in oil, drained

1 tsp salted capers

3 tbsp olive oil

1 tbsp sherry vinegar

1 tsp Dijon mustard

salt and pepper

500 g/1 lb 2 oz fresh clams

about 175 ml/6 fl oz water

500 g/1 lb 2 oz broad beans,
    shelled if fresh

2 tbsp chopped mixed fresh
    herbs, such as parsley,
    chives and mint

method

1 Place the anchovies in a small bowl, then add water to cover and soak for 5 minutes. Drain well, then pat dry with kitchen paper and place in a mortar. Brush the salt off the capers, then add to the mortar and pound to a paste with a pestle.

2 Whisk the olive oil, vinegar and mustard together in a separate bowl, then whisk in the anchovy paste and season to taste with pepper. Cover with clingfilm and stand at room temperature until required.

3 Scrub the clams under cold running water. Discard any with broken shells or any that do not close immediately when sharply tapped. Place the clams in a large saucepan and add the water. Cover and bring to the boil over high heat. Cook, shaking the pan occasionally, for 3–5 minutes or until the clams have opened. Discard any that remain closed.

4 Bring a large saucepan of lightly salted water to the boil. Add the broad beans, then return to the boil and blanch for 5 minutes. Drain, then refresh under cold running water and drain again. Remove and discard the outer skins and place the broad beans in a bowl.

5 Drain the clams and remove them from their shells. Add to the beans and sprinkle with the herbs. Add the anchovy vinaigrette and toss lightly. Serve warm.

# of eggs and cheese

Egg-based dishes feature in all tapas menus, and one of the most familiar of these is the delectable Spanish Tortilla – made hearty with the addition of chunks of waxy potato, this is definitely an omelette with attitude! The potatoes can be boiled before being mixed with the eggs, but to make a really authentic tortilla they are first cooked slowly in a generous quantity of olive oil so that they absorb the flavour of the oil but do not become browned or crisp, or fall apart. This chapter includes a recipe for the simplest – and perhaps the best – of tortillas, as well as a few with added extras. There are also recipes for other ways of using eggs – devilled, fried, scrambled and oven-baked. With their exotic names, such as Flamenco Eggs and Basque Scrambled Eggs, these dishes conjure up wonderful images of Spain.

Cheese dishes are also popular in tapas menus, and some very tempting recipes are given here. If you really want to impress, serve an intriguing combination of fresh figs, crumbly blue cheese and caramelized almonds. Or try melt-in-the-mouth cheese puffs with a fiery salsa, or tiny empanadillas filled with cheese and olives. It can be difficult to find Spanish cheese on sale in other countries, so alternatives are suggested in case you are unable to source the real thing.

tortilla española

ingredients

SERVES 8

450 ml/12 fl oz Spanish
   olive oil

450 g/1 lb waxy potatoes,
   cubed

2 onions, chopped

2 large eggs

salt and pepper

sprigs of fresh flat-leaf
   parsley, to garnish

method

1 Heat the olive oil in a large, heavy-based frying pan. Add the potato cubes and onions, then lower the heat and cook, stirring frequently so that the potatoes do not clump together, for 20 minutes or until tender but not browned. Place a sieve over a large bowl and drain the potatoes and onions well. Set aside the oil.

2 Beat the eggs lightly in a large bowl and season well with salt and pepper. Gently stir in the potatoes and onions.

3 Wipe out the frying pan with kitchen paper and heat 2 tablespoons of the reserved olive oil. When hot, add the egg and potato mixture, lower the heat and cook for 3–5 minutes or until the underside is just set. Use a spatula to submerge the potatoes in the egg and loosen the tortilla from the bottom of the frying pan to stop it sticking.

4 Cover the tortilla with a plate and hold the plate in place with the other hand. Drain off the oil in the frying pan, then quickly invert the tortilla onto the plate. Return the frying pan to the heat and add a little more oil if necessary. Slide the tortilla, cooked side uppermost, back into the frying pan and cook for a further 3–5 minutes or until set underneath.

5 Slide the tortilla onto a serving plate and let stand for about 15 minutes. Serve warm or cold, garnished with parsley sprigs.

chorizo & cheese tortilla

ingredients

SERVES 8

2 small potatoes

4 tbsp olive oil

1 small onion, chopped

1 red pepper, deseeded
  and chopped

2 tomatoes, deseeded and
  diced

140 g/5 oz chorizo sausage,
  finely chopped

8 large eggs

2 tbsp cold water

salt and pepper

55 g/2 oz mature Mahon,
  Manchego, or Parmesan
  cheese, grated

method

1 Cook the potatoes in a small pan of lightly salted boiling water for 15–20 minutes or until just tender. Drain and set aside until cool enough to handle, then dice.

2 Heat the olive oil in a large frying pan that can safely be placed under the grill. Add the onion, pepper and tomatoes and cook over low heat, stirring occasionally, for 5 minutes. Add the diced potatoes and chorizo and cook for a further 5 minutes. Meanwhile, preheat the grill to high.

3 Beat the eggs with the water and salt and pepper to taste in a large bowl. Pour the mixture into the frying pan and cook for 8–10 minutes or until the underside is set. Lift the edge of the tortilla occasionally to let the uncooked egg run underneath. Sprinkle the grated cheese over the tortilla and place under the hot grill for 3 minutes or until the top is set and the cheese has melted. Serve, warm or cold, cut into thin wedges.

spinach & mushroom tortilla

ingredients

SERVES 4

2 tbsp olive oil

3 shallots, finely chopped

350 g/12 oz mushrooms, sliced

280 g/10 oz fresh spinach
leaves, coarse stems
removed

salt and pepper

55 g/2 oz toasted flaked
almonds

5 eggs

2 tbsp chopped fresh parsley

2 tbsp cold water

85 g/3 oz mature Mahon,
Manchego, or Parmesan
cheese, grated

method

1 Heat the olive oil in a frying pan that can safely be placed under the grill. Add the shallots and cook over low heat, stirring occasionally, for 5 minutes or until softened. Add the mushrooms and cook, stirring frequently, for a further 4 minutes. Add the spinach, then increase the heat to medium and cook, stirring frequently, for 3–4 minutes or until wilted. Reduce the heat, then season to taste with salt and pepper and stir in the flaked almonds.

2 Beat the eggs with the parsley, water and salt and pepper to taste in a bowl. Pour the mixture into the frying pan and cook for 5–8 minutes or until the underside is set. Lift the edge of the tortilla occasionally to let the uncooked egg run underneath. Meanwhile, preheat the grill to high.

3 Sprinkle the grated cheese over the tortilla and cook under the preheated hot grill for 3 minutes or until the top is set and the cheese has melted. Serve, lukewarm or cold, cut into thin wedges.

oven-baked tortilla

ingredients

MAKES 48

olive oil

1 large garlic clove, crushed

4 spring onions, white and
    green parts finely chopped

1 green pepper, deseeded
    and finely diced

1 red pepper, deseeded
    and finely diced

175 g/6 oz potato, boiled,
    peeled and diced

5 large eggs

100 ml/3$\frac{1}{2}$ fl oz sour cream

175 g/6 oz freshly grated
    Spanish Roncal cheese,
    or Cheddar or Parmesan
    cheese

3 tbsp snipped fresh chives

salt and pepper

salad leaves, to serve

method

1 Preheat the oven to 190°C/375°F. Line an 18 x 25-cm/7 x 10-inch baking tin with foil and brush with the olive oil. Reserve.

2 Place a little olive oil, the garlic, spring onions and peppers in a frying pan and cook over medium heat, stirring, for 10 minutes or until the onions are softened but not browned. Set aside to cool, then stir in the potato.

3 Beat the eggs, sour cream, cheese and chives together in a large bowl. Stir the cooled vegetables into the bowl and season to taste with salt and pepper.

4 Pour the mixture into the baking tin and smooth over the top. Bake in the preheated oven for 30–40 minutes or until golden brown, puffed and set in the centre. Remove from the oven and set aside to cool. Run a spatula around the edge, then invert onto a cutting board, browned-side up, and peel off the foil. If the surface looks a little runny, place it under a medium grill to dry out.

5 Set aside to cool completely. Trim the edges if necessary, then cut into 48 squares. Serve on a platter with wooden cocktail sticks or secure each square to a slice of bread. Accompany with salad leaves.

stuffed eggs

ingredients

SERVES 6

6 hard-boiled eggs,
    cooled and shelled
120 g/4^1/$_4$ oz canned
    sardines in olive oil,
    drained
4 tbsp lemon juice
dash of Tabasco sauce
1–2 tbsp mayonnaise
salt and pepper
55 g/2 oz plain flour
85 g/3 oz fresh white
    breadcrumbs
1 large egg, lightly beaten
vegetable oil, for deep-frying
fresh parsley sprigs,
    to garnish

method

1 Cut the eggs in half lengthways and, using a teaspoon, carefully scoop out the yolks into a fine sieve, reserving the egg white halves. Rub the yolks through the sieve into a bowl.

2 Mash the sardines with a fork, then mix with the egg yolks. Stir in the lemon juice and Tabasco, then add enough mayonnaise to make a paste. Season to taste with salt and pepper.

3 Spoon the filling into the egg white halves, mounding it up well. Spread out the flour and breadcrumbs in separate shallow dishes. Dip each egg half first in the flour, then in the beaten egg and finally in the breadcrumbs.

4 Heat the vegetable oil for deep-frying in a deep-fat fryer or large pan to 180–190°C/ 350–375°F, or until a cube of bread browns in 30 seconds. Deep-fry the egg halves, in batches if necessary, for 2 minutes or until golden brown. Drain on kitchen paper and serve hot, garnished with parsley sprigs.

devilled eggs

ingredients

MAKES 16

8 large eggs

2 whole pimientos from a jar
   or can

8 green olives

5 tbsp mayonnaise

8 drops Tabasco sauce

large pinch cayenne pepper

salt and pepper

paprika, for dusting

sprigs of fresh dill, to garnish

method

1 To cook the eggs, put them in a saucepan, cover with cold water and slowly bring to the boil. Immediately reduce the heat to very low, cover and simmer gently for 10 minutes. As soon as the eggs are cooked, drain and put under cold running water to prevent a black ring from forming round the yolk. Gently tap the eggs to crack the shells and set aside until cold. When cold, remove the shells.

2 Using a stainless steel knife, halve the eggs lengthways, then carefully remove the yolks. Put the yolks in a nylon sieve set over a bowl and rub through, then mash them with a wooden spoon or fork. If necessary, rinse the egg whites under cold water and dry very carefully.

3 Drain the pimientos on kitchen paper, then chop them finely, reserving a few strips. Finely chop the olives, reserving 16 larger pieces to garnish. Add the chopped pimientos and chopped olives to the mashed egg yolks. Add the mayonnaise, mix well together, then add the Tabasco sauce, cayenne pepper and salt and pepper to taste.

4 Use a teaspoon to spoon the prepared filling into each egg half. Arrange the eggs on a serving plate. Add a small strip of the reserved pimientos and a piece of olive to the top of each stuffed egg. Dust with a little paprika and garnish with dill sprigs.

eggs & cheese

ingredients

SERVES 6

6 hard-boiled eggs, cooled
   and shelled

3 tbsp grated Manchego or
   Cheddar cheese

1–2 tbsp mayonnaise

2 tbsp snipped fresh chives

1 fresh red chilli, deseeded
   and finely chopped

salt and pepper

lettuce leaves, to serve

method

1 Cut the eggs in half lengthways and, using a teaspoon, carefully scoop out the yolks into a fine sieve, reserving the egg white halves. Rub the yolks through the sieve into a bowl and add the grated cheese, mayonnaise, chives, chilli, salt and pepper. Spoon the filling into the egg white halves.

2 Arrange a bed of lettuce on individual serving plates and top with the eggs. Cover and chill until ready to serve.

flamenco eggs

ingredients

SERVES 4

4 tbsp olive oil

1 onion, thinly sliced

2 garlic cloves,
    finely chopped

2 small red peppers,
    deseeded and chopped

4 tomatoes, peeled, deseeded
    and chopped

1 tbsp chopped fresh parsley

salt and cayenne pepper

200 g/7 oz canned
    sweetcorn, drained

4 eggs

method

1 Preheat the oven to 180°C/350°F. Heat the olive oil in a large, heavy-based frying pan. Add the onion and garlic and cook over low heat, stirring occasionally, for 5 minutes or until softened. Add the red peppers and cook, stirring occasionally, for a further 10 minutes. Stir in the tomatoes and parsley, season to taste with salt and cayenne and cook for a further 5 minutes. Stir in the sweetcorn and remove the pan from the heat.

2 Divide the mixture between 4 individual ovenproof dishes. Make a hollow in the surface of each using the back of a spoon. Break an egg into each depression.

3 Bake in the preheated oven for 15–25 minutes or until the eggs have set. Serve hot.

basque scrambled eggs

ingredients

SERVES 4–6

3–4 tbsp olive oil

1 large onion, finely chopped

1 large red pepper, deseeded
and chopped

1 large green pepper,
deseeded and chopped

2 large tomatoes, peeled,
deseeded and chopped

55 g/2 oz chorizo sausage,
sliced thinly, outer casing
removed, if preferred

35 g/1$^1/_4$ oz butter

10 large eggs, lightly beaten

salt and pepper

4–6 thick slices country-style
bread, toasted, to serve

method

1 Heat 2 tablespoons of olive oil in a large, heavy-based frying pan over medium heat. Add the onion and peppers and cook for 5 minutes or until the vegetables are softened but not browned. Add the tomatoes and heat through. Transfer to a heatproof plate and keep warm in a preheated low oven.

2 Add another tablespoon of oil to the frying pan. Add the chorizo and cook for 30 seconds, just to warm through and flavour the oil. Add the chorizo to the reserved vegetables.

3 Add a little extra olive oil, if necessary, to bring it back to 2 tablespoons. Add the butter and let it melt. Season the eggs with salt and pepper, then add to the frying pan and scramble until cooked to the desired degree of firmness. Return the vegetables to the pan and stir through. Serve immediately with hot toast.

chorizo & quail's eggs

ingredients

MAKES 12

12 slices French bread, sliced
    on the diagonal, about
    5 mm/$1/4$ inch thick
40 g/$11/2$ oz cured,
    ready-to-eat chorizo,
    cut into 12 thin slices
olive oil
12 quail's eggs
mild paprika
salt and pepper
fresh flat-leaf parsley,
    to garnish

method

1 Preheat the grill to high. Arrange the slices of bread on a baking sheet and grill until golden brown on both sides.

2 Cut or fold the chorizo slices to fit on the toasts, then reserve.

3 Heat a thin layer of olive oil in a large frying pan over medium heat until a cube of bread sizzles – about 40 seconds. Break the eggs into the frying pan and cook, spooning the fat over the yolks, until the whites are set and the yolks are cooked to your liking.

4 Remove the fried eggs from the frying pan and drain on kitchen paper. Immediately transfer to the chorizo-topped toasts and dust with paprika. Season to taste with salt and pepper, then garnish with parsley and serve immediately.

deep-fried manchego cheese

ingredients

SERVES 6–8

200 g/7 oz Manchego cheese

3 tbsp plain flour

salt and pepper

1 egg

1 tsp water

85 g/3 oz fresh white or
    brown breadcrumbs

corn oil, for deep-frying

method

1 Slice the cheese into triangular shapes about 2 cm/2/3 inch thick. Put the flour in a plastic bag and season with salt and pepper to taste. Break the egg into a shallow dish and beat together with the water. Spread out the breadcrumbs on a plate.

2 Toss the cheese pieces in the flour so that they are evenly coated, then dip the cheese in the egg mixture. Finally, dip the cheese in the breadcrumbs so that the pieces are coated on all sides.

3 Just before serving, heat about 2.5 cm/ 1 inch of the corn oil in a large, heavy-based frying pan or heat the oil in a deep-fryer to 180–190°C/350–375°F or until a cube of bread browns in 30 seconds. Add the cheese pieces, in batches of about 4 or 5 pieces so that the temperature of the oil does not drop, and deep-fry for 1–2 minutes, turning once, until the cheese is just starting to melt and they are golden brown on all sides. Do make sure that the oil is hot enough, otherwise the coating on the cheese will take too long to become crisp and the cheese inside may ooze out.

4 Using a slotted spoon, remove the cheese from the frying pan or deep-fryer and drain well on kitchen paper. Serve hot.

cheese puffs with fiery tomato salsa

ingredients

SERVES 8

70 g/2¹/₂ oz plain flour

50 ml/2 fl oz Spanish olive oil

150 ml/5 fl oz water

2 eggs, beaten

55 g/2 oz Manchego,
      Parmesan, Cheddar,
      Gouda or Gruyère cheese,
      finely grated

¹/₂ tsp paprika

salt and pepper

corn oil, for deep-frying

fiery tomato salsa

2 tbsp Spanish olive oil

1 small onion, finely chopped

1 garlic clove, crushed

splash of dry white wine

400 g/14 oz canned chopped
      tomatoes

1 tbsp tomato purée

¹/₄–¹/₂ tsp dried red pepper
      flakes

dash of Tabasco sauce

pinch of sugar

salt and pepper

method

1 To make the salsa, heat the olive oil in a saucepan, add the onion and cook until softened but not browned. Add the garlic and cook for 30 seconds. Add the wine and let it bubble, then add the remaining salsa ingredients and simmer, uncovered, until a thick sauce is formed. Set aside.

2 Meanwhile, prepare the cheese puffs. Sift the flour onto a plate. Put the olive oil and water in a pan and slowly bring to the boil. As soon as the water boils, remove the pan from the heat and quickly tip in the flour. Using a wooden spoon, beat the mixture well until it is smooth and leaves the sides of the pan.

3 Cool for 1–2 minutes, then gradually add the eggs, beating hard after each addition and keeping the mixture stiff. Add the cheese and paprika, season to taste with salt and pepper and mix well together.

4 To cook the cheese puffs, heat the corn oil in a deep-fryer to 180–190°C/350–375°F. Drop teaspoonfuls of the prepared mixture, in batches, into the hot oil and deep-fry for 2–3 minutes, turning once, or until golden and crispy. They should rise to the surface of the oil and puff up. Drain well on kitchen paper. Serve the puffs piping hot, with the fiery salsa.

figs with blue cheese

ingredients

SERVES 6

12 ripe figs

350 g/12 oz Spanish blue
    cheese, such as Picos,
    crumbled

extra-virgin olive oil, to serve

caramelized almonds

100 g/3$\frac{1}{2}$ oz caster sugar

115 g/4 oz whole almonds

butter, for greasing

method

1 First make the caramelized almonds. Place the sugar in a saucepan over medium heat and stir until the sugar melts and turns golden brown and bubbles. Do not stir once the mixture begins to bubble. Remove the pan from the heat, then add the almonds one at a time and quickly turn with a fork until coated. If the caramel hardens, return the pan to the heat. Transfer each almond to a lightly greased baking sheet once it is coated. Set aside until cool and firm.

2 To serve, slice the figs in half and arrange 4 halves on individual serving plates. Roughly chop the almonds by hand. Place a mound of blue cheese on each plate and sprinkle with chopped almonds. Drizzle the figs very lightly with the olive oil.

bean & cabrales salad

ingredients

SERVES 4

150 g/5^{1}/$_{2}$ oz small dried
    cannellini beans, soaked
    for 4 hours or overnight

1 bay leaf

4 tbsp olive oil

2 tbsp sherry vinegar

2 tsp clear honey

1 tsp dijon mustard

salt and pepper

2 tbsp toasted flaked almonds

200 g/7 oz Cabrales or other
    blue cheese, crumbled

method

1 Drain the beans and place in a large, heavy-based saucepan. Pour in enough water to cover, then add the bay leaf and bring to the boil. Boil for 1–1^{1}/$_{2}$ hours or until tender. Drain, then tip into a bowl and cool slightly. Remove and discard the bay leaf.

2 Meanwhile, make the dressing. Whisk the olive oil, vinegar, honey and mustard together in a bowl and season to taste with salt and pepper. Pour the dressing over the beans and toss lightly. Add the almonds and toss lightly again. Cool to room temperature.

3 To serve, spoon the beans into individual serving bowls and scatter over the cheese.

cheese & shallots with herb dressing

ingredients

SERVES 6

1 tsp sesame seeds

$1/4$ tsp cumin seeds

4 tomatoes, deseeded
    and diced

5 tbsp olive oil

4 tbsp lemon juice

salt and pepper

2 tsp chopped fresh thyme

1 tbsp chopped fresh mint

4 shallots, finely chopped

500 g/1 lb 2 oz Idiazabal or
    other sheep's milk
    cheese, diced

method

1 Dry-fry the sesame and cumin seeds in a small, heavy-based frying pan, shaking the pan frequently, until they begin to pop and give off their aroma. Remove from the heat and set aside to cool.

2 Place the tomatoes in a bowl. To make the dressing, whisk the olive oil and lemon juice together in a separate bowl. Season to taste with salt and pepper, then add the thyme, mint and shallots and mix well.

3 Place the cheese in another bowl. Pour half the dressing over the tomatoes and toss lightly. Cover with clingfilm and chill for 1 hour. Pour the remaining dressing over the cheese, then cover and chill for 1 hour.

4 To serve, divide the cheese mixture between 6 serving plates and sprinkle with half the toasted seeds. Top with the tomato mixture and sprinkle with the remaining toasted seeds.

roasted peppers with fiery cheese

ingredients

SERVES 6

1 red pepper, halved
    and deseeded

1 orange pepper, halved
    and deseeded

1 yellow pepper, halved
    and deseeded

115 g/4 oz Afuega'l Pitu
    cheese or other hot spiced
    cheese, diced

1 tbsp clear honey

1 tbsp sherry vinegar

salt and pepper

method

1 Preheat the grill to high. Place the peppers, skin-side up, in a single layer on a baking sheet. Cook under the hot grill for 8–10 minutes or until the skins have blistered and blackened. Using tongs, transfer to a plastic bag. Tie the top and set aside to cool.

2 When the peppers are cool enough to handle, peel off the skin with your fingers or a knife and discard it. Place on a serving plate and sprinkle over the cheese.

3 Whisk the honey and vinegar together in a bowl and season to taste with salt and pepper. Pour the dressing over the peppers, then cover and chill until required.

burgos with sherry vinegar

ingredients

SERVES 4

400 g/14 oz Burgos cheese

1–2 tbsp clear honey

3 tbsp sherry vinegar

carrot sticks

chilled sherry, to serve

method

1 Place the cheese in a bowl and beat until smooth, then beat in 1 tablespoon of the honey and 1^1/$_2$ tablespoons of the vinegar.

2 Taste and adjust the sweetness to taste by adding more honey or more vinegar as required.

3 Divide between 4 small serving bowls, then cover and chill until required. Serve with carrot sticks and chilled sherry.

cheese & olive empanadillas

ingredients

MAKES 26

85 g/3 oz firm or soft cheese

85 g/3 oz pitted green olives

55 g/2 oz sundried tomatoes
    in oil, drained

50 g/1¾ oz canned
    anchovies, drained

pepper

2 tbsp sundried tomato purée

plain flour, for dusting

500 g/1 lb 2 oz ready-made
    puff pastry, thawed
    if frozen

beaten egg, to glaze

fresh flat-leaf parsley sprigs,
    to garnish

method

1 Preheat the oven to 400°F/200°C. Cut the cheese into small dice measuring about 5 mm/¼ inch. Chop the olives, sundried tomatoes and anchovies into pieces about the same size as the cheese. Put all the chopped ingredients in a bowl, season with pepper to taste and gently mix together. Stir in the sundried tomato purée.

2 On a lightly floured work surface, thinly roll out the puff pastry. Using a plain, round 8-cm/3¼-inch cutter, cut into 18 circles. Gently pile the trimmings together, roll out again, then cut out an additional 8 circles. Using a teaspoon, put a little of the prepared filling in the centre of each circle.

3 Dampen the edges of the pastry with a little water, then bring up the sides to cover the filling completely and pinch the edges together with your fingers to seal them. With the tip of a sharp knife, make a small slit in the top of each pastry. You can store the pastries in the refrigerator at this stage until you are ready to bake them.

4 Place the pastries onto dampened baking sheets and brush each with a little beaten egg to glaze. Bake in the oven for 10–15 minutes or until golden brown, crisp and well risen. Serve the empanadillas piping hot, warm or cold, garnished with parsley sprigs.